COLLECTED POEMS
1933–1973

Books by ALLEN CURNOW
other than the volumes of poetry
incorporated in this volume

A Book of New Zealand Verse (editor) 1945
The Axe, a Verse Tragedy 1949
The Penguin Book of New Zealand Verse (editor) 1960
Four Plays 1972

COLLECTED POEMS
1933–1973

Allen Curnow

A.H. & A.W. REED
Wellington Sydney London

First published 1974

A. H. & A. W. REED LTD
182 Wakefield Street, Wellington
51 Whiting Street, Artarmon, NSW 2064
11 Southampton Row, London WC1B 5HA
also
29 Dacre Street, Auckland
165 Cashel Street, Christchurch

© 1974 Allen Curnow

All rights reserved. No part of this publication may be reproduced, stored in a retrieval system or transmitted in any form or by any means electronic, mechanical, photocopying, recording or otherwise without the prior written permission of the publishers.

ISBN 0 589 00826 9

Library of Congress Catalogue Card No. 73-85434

Printed by New Zealand Consolidated Press Limited, Wellington.

To Jeny

Among these poems are some which have appeared in *The Press* (Christchurch, NZ), *Landfall, Islands,* the *New Zealand Listener, Meanjin Papers, Poetry Quarterly, Folios of New Writing, Penguin New Writing, Poetry London, Poetry* (Chicago), *New World Writing* (New York), and the *Times Literary Supplement* (London). To all these acknowledgment is made.

The collections *Trees, Effigies, Moving Objects* and *An Abominable Temper* were first published by the Catspaw Press, Wellington, to which, and to Mr Denis Glover, I acknowledge my debt.

A.C.

CONTENTS

AUTHOR'S NOTE — xii

VALLEY OF DECISION 1933
- Sea Changes — 3
- Renunciation — 4
- Et resurrexit — 5
- Venture — 6
- Valley of Decision — 7
- At the Brink — 8
- Matins — 9
- His Deceit — 10
- Four Walls — 11
- Behold now Behemoth — 12
- The Spirit Shall Return — 13
- The Agony — 14
- Screened — 15
- Host of the Air — 16
- Status quo — 17
- The Serpent — 18
- Apocalyptic — 19
- Power of the Many — 20
- On Relief — 21

THREE POEMS 1935
- Aspects of Monism — 25
- Restraint — 27
- The Wilderness — 28

ENEMIES 1937
- New Zealand City — 31
- Recall to Earth — 33
- Chief End — 34
- Factory at Night — 35
- Colonial Outlook — 36
- A Woman in Mind — 37
- Mountain Elegy — 41

CONTENTS CONTINUED

Enemies	43
Slum	44
Remainder	46
Orbit	47
The Leaves Dead	48
Paid Well	49

NOT IN NARROW SEAS 1939

Dedication	53
Statement	55
I The water is burred with rain	57
II Eighty years since salted sails	58
III Strut on the beach loos'd nervous limbs	59
IV Escape in seeming from smoke and iron	60
V Blood in the climbing limb	61
VI The bishop boundary-rides his diocese	63
VII Woman who wakes beneath casewood and canvas	64
VIII Child of the stolen country	65
IX Haul the flag to the top of the mast	67
X Jaunty hopes that play	69
XI Naked goes the land	71
XII Where Van Gogh struck his seed	73
Epilogue	74

ISLAND AND TIME 1941

Sentence	78
The Unhistoric Story	79
The Dance	81
Fantasy on a Hillside	82
Time	83
Dry Weather	84
St Thomas's Ruins	85
Time and the Child	86
Song	88
Polar Outlook	90
House and Land	91
The Scene	93
Morning Moon	96
Expect No Settlements	97
Crash at Leithfield	98
Quick One in Summer	100
Lake Mapourika	101
Country School	102
A Victim	103

CONTENTS CONTINUED

Sestina	105
Wild Iron	107
Second Song	108
It Is Too Late	109
Dialogue of Island and Time	111
No Second Coming	116

SAILING OR DROWNING 1943
Discovery	119
Nine Sonnets	120
I In Memoriam 2/Lt T.C.F. Ronalds	120
II Out of Sleep	121
III Sailing or Drowning	122
IV Polynesia	123
V The Navigators	124
VI The Fall of Icarus	125
VII The Old Provincial Council Buildings, Christchurch	126
VIII To M. H. Holcroft	127
IX At Joachim Kahn's	128
Spring, 1942	129
Rite of Spring	132
In Summer Sheeted Under	133
Pantoum of War in the Pacific	134
Landfall in Unknown Seas	136
Attitudes for a New Zealand Poet	140
I That part of you the world offended so	140
II World, up to now we've heard your hungers wail	141
III The Skeleton of the Great Moa in the Canterbury Museum, Christchurch	142

JACK WITHOUT MAGIC 1946
Jack Without Magic	145
Dimensional	146
Children, Swimmers	147
Paradise Revisited	148
Self-portrait	149
The Waking Bird Refutes	150
Unhurt, There is No Help	151
Dunedin	152
To D.G. Overseas	153
Darkness, Patience	154

AT DEAD LOW WATER 1949
At Dead Low Water	157

CONTENTS CONTINUED

Tomb of an Ancestor   160
- I In Memoriam R. L. M. G.   160
- II To Fanny Rose May   161

Four Descriptions and a Picture   162
- I Genesis   162
- II With How Mad Steps   163
- III She Sits with Her Two Children   164
- IV Then If This Dies   165
- V All Darkens But Her Image   166

Old Hand of the Sea   167
Eden Gate   168
Music for Words   169
Lili Kraus Playing at Christchurch   170
A Sonata of Schubert   171

POEMS 1949-1957   1957

A Leaf   175
To Forget Self and All   176
Idylls in Colour Film   177
- I Cristobal   177
- II Curacao   179

Elegy on My Father   180
When the Hulk of the World   182
The Eye Is More Or Less Satisfied with Seeing   183
In Memory of Dylan Thomas   184
Keep in a Cool Place   188
To Introduce the Landscape   189
Jack-in-the-Boat   190
Mementos of an Occasion   191
Spectacular Blossom   193
Evidences of Recent Flood   194
- I Logbook Found on Ararat   194
- II The Changeling   197

He Cracked a Word   200

A SMALL ROOM WITH LARGE WINDOWS   1962

A Small Room with Large Windows   203
An Oppressive Climate, a Populous Neighbourhood   205

TREES, EFFIGIES, MOVING OBJECTS   1972

- I Lone Kauri Road   211
- II Friendship Heights   213
- III An Upper Room   215
- IV Agenda   216

CONTENTS CONTINUED

V	Do It Yourself	217
VI	Names Are News	218
VII	A Family Matter	221
VIII	The Kitchen Cupboard	222
IX	A Dead Lamb	223
X	A Framed Photograph	224
XI	Two Pedestrians with One Thought	226
XII	Magnificat	228
XIII	A Four Letter Word	230
XIV	Bourdon	233
XV	A Hot Time	234
XVI	There Is a Pleasure in the Pathless Woods	236
XVII	Lone Kauri Road	237
XVIII	Any Time Now	238

AN ABOMINABLE TEMPER 1973

To the Reader	241
A Window Frame	242
To an Unfortunate Young Lady	244
This Beach Can Be Dangerous	245
To Douglas Lilburn at Fifty	246
What Was That?	248
A Refusal to Read Poems of James K. Baxter at a Performance in Honour of his Memory	250
Tantalus	251
An Abominable Temper	252

NOTES   263

AUTHOR'S NOTE

NINETEEN of the twenty-two poems in my earliest volume *Valley of Decision* appear in this book, all of them revised. It may be as rash to revise in my sixty-third year what I wrote between my eighteenth and my twenty-first, as it was to publish them in the first place. I do not know that that is a serious objection. All poems are rash acts, and no less so — more, perhaps — for the deliberate care one takes. Even after forty years some poems carry between or under the lines their own instructions for revision. These instructions a poet must read as well as he can. His choice is between ignoring them and acting on them, and if he acts, he takes the risk of exceeding them. I think it is a good risk to take. If he doesn't revise, he is in effect concealing something from the reader: some part of his own better understanding.

Discontent, even disgust, with their earliest work is the common experience of poets. It is a mood. Moods don't help much, when it comes to the question: do I, or do I not, wish to suppress — or disown, since I cannot suppress — this part of my writing? I have to answer for *this* poet, myself, never mind what might be best for another. The impulse to revise, of itself, gives the answer. These earliest poems — like those in *Enemies* and *Three Poems*, which I have also revised here and there — have their place with all that I have written since. A hundred years ago, a conscientious editor might have covered all this with the disarming subtitle *Juvenilia*. That would not be suitable here, even if it were possible; there are too many connexions between my earliest and my latest poems to justify such a separation; they must stand together, for better or worse.

None of these early poems has been an anthologist's favourite, so the revisions should upset nobody. I do not call attention to them because I imagine many readers will notice them, but because I am accountable to the few who will. Having done so, I remember that there are famous instances of a poet's revising his life — correcting youthful beliefs or opinions — in touching up his early writings. There is no critical appeal against this, as a poet's own verdict on his work. In my case, it would be a futile exercise. In *Valley of Decision,* and after it, some crisis or change from faith to scepticism may be read, however perplexed and precarious the faith was, and the scepticism no less so. No revision can alter this. Whatever the life has been — and who knows very much about that? — the poetry is all one book.

I have altered almost nothing in *Not in Narrow Seas*. It has its own accent. It sets its own limits of a time and a place with a peculiar severity. I suppose it could be called my contribution to the anti-myth about New Zealand which a few of us poets — and almost nobody else — were so busy making in those years. It had to be done. The country did not know what to make of itself, colony or nation, privileged happyland or miserable banishment: the polarisation was nothing new, and it is still with us, but we were the first to find poetry in it. I know that I wanted, for myself, to focus the vision sharply on a few details of a few scenes of New Zealand history, some of them distinct to me from childhood. I had not the sense of a poetic style, ready for use, that my elders Mason and Fairburn had; I had to improvise one for myself; but we had in common that instinct for a few particulars, sharpened by our antipathy to almost everything that satisfied — or seemed to satisfy — an older generation. I shared the antipathy, of course, with Denis Glover: each, in those days, wished he could write like the other, the last thing either of us could ever have done. Very soon after, I was writing the poems of *Island and Time* and *Sailing or Drowning*. I had to get past the severities, not to say rigidities, of our New Zealand anti-myth: away from questions which present themselves as public and answerable, towards the questions which are always private and unanswerable. The geographical anxieties didn't disappear; but I began to find a personal and poetic use for them, rather than let them use me up.

About the poems of the last thirty years I should have nothing to say here. They are the best I can do, so far; the little of the little I know, of myself and my world, that I have tried to add to the limitless disclosures, or inventions, that we call by the name of poetry. A collection on this scale will please, or displease, in different ways and places. Having made it, I must not make too much of it. I hope I have not finished yet.

The poem 'At Dead Low Water' first appeared in *Jack Without Magic*. I have placed it here in the later volume of which it became the title-poem. Similarly, I have placed 'A Small Room with Large Windows' in the volume which bears that title, not in *Poems 1949-1957* where it was first collected.

VALLEY OF DECISION
1933

SEA CHANGES

Strange times have taken hold on me,
strange seas have locked across my eyes,
thick in the twilight undersea
unheard-of silence heard these cries.

Out of the glimmer of green waters
the ringing deafness of dark seas,
such dim-begotten sons and daughters
of love and cold-flesh death are these:

Uncertain are they hunting on
and all their faith's inconstancy;
they are who touch and straight are gone
yet have no other where to be.

RENUNCIATION

Darken, eyes, toward the day,
look well on neither flower nor tree:
I have given a springing world away
for worlds which I believe to be.

The motion of this ill belief
I cannot speak, lest every word
whine to a soft attenuate grief
and every flower burn out a sword

surgeon's or angel's keen to cut
body from soul, one two, one two.
Eyes, darken; whining mouth, be shut
till I have cleaner work for you.

ET RESURREXIT

Servants of God,
how do you stand
to their witness,
eye, ear, hand?

Eternal heaven
as the eye can see
is wing's upon wing's
tautology.

As the ear can hear
there is no song
but of brute birth
and mortal tongue.

All the hand knows
for a fast friend
is blind first touch
and a last as blind.

How does that heaven
of yours agree
with this, life's in-
most certainty?

We teach it this way,
sons of men:
on the third day
He rose again.

VENTURE

He had begun to look within
and midnight high the walls flew up,
God was a breath of blazing cold
before the morning winds begin:

and now he was a timeless king,
now dust of all kings ever rode
over such walls and dropped their dead
and knew they were not anything:

now rounding eye on eye he saw
the breathless builder on the walls,
the blazing cold, the towering bone
was God within as God before.

'Be damned these aching walls' he said,
'be sunk this fire to natural hell.
'I looked within, only to find
'what eyes are pricking in my head.'

So he went by and looked without,
to find the old and equal sight,
but there was fog and a few stones,
a dazed wind puffed the dust about,

and a strange face he knew was cold
(so white) said to him with half lips,
'Now you have learned to look within
'there's nothing here that is not old.'

He saw the steep flight of the wall,
the blazing cold, the breath of God:
now king, now dust, whatever's crushed
between the thumb and the eyeball.

VALLEY OF DECISION

Come to the cliff, look over,
see your years flake down,
man, you'll discover
truth is a ghost town

fallen out of time
from this cliff top,
truth is the dizzy climb,
the sheer drop.

Proud hour, creeping minute
flake, fall, strew
the ghostly polis, in it
your lies come true;

hopes, loves, reasons,
times of your life,
all weathers and seasons
shredded over the knife

edge of this chasm —
shape and substance
a twitch of the eye, a spasm,
a dusty dance

idly neither here nor
there, a breath
trapped, do you need more
to please death?

Come to the cliff, look over,
see your years flake down,
man, you'll discover
truth is a ghost town.

AT THE BRINK

When I have seen a perfect flower
or stood a little by the sea
love on this beauty there begets
the pain of clouded sight in me;

for perfect things must needs be dead
or live alone in perfect praise,
and one bright day is but the seal
of countless deaths of countless days.

The poets and their nightingales
both sing, two voices in one song;
but matched against eternity
the music does not echo long.

Can there be light beyond the day,
the common sun of lovely things?
Beauty's a creature of the mind.
No nightingale, but poet, sings.

Beauty's a tree that walks by night,
the farthest sentinel of sense,
dark hope of an enduring light
in an eternal transience.

MATINS

Pray God and quiet take
for this day's part
of His desiring, make
greater your heart

to brim the joy and shame
the hours repeat
as Light in pity's name
kneels at your feet

and sues you, offering
quick love before you:
birds at your rising sing:
angels adore you.

He gives you suns to burn:
beauty for beauty
give then, your best return
candles for duty.

HIS DECEIT

And so the world makes you unquiet too,
so cold upon your pride of being man:
you too have thought how there is nothing new
under the sun, since under-sun began;

so you lean hard upon your hands in prayer,
your grace of life, your fleshhood all denied
saying, 'Lord, indeed for these I have no care.'
God in his beauty curse you for your pride.

FOUR WALLS

The street's a fixed stare on the pointless night
black focus of the nearest dark, direct
sharp style of limits whose shrewd architect
shaped in the circling flux of mortal sight

a walled city against the infinite ways
where spirits mount nor ever make an end
of star on star, high towers to defend
our finished hours and finely rounded days:

these are brave walls about our narrow peace,
between them measured seconds rule our feet;
the swinging littleness we pace nor cease
to labour comfort from our spare deceit:

yet star on star the motion of ascent
shadows across the difficult content.

BEHOLD NOW BEHEMOTH

See the wide-footed, pendant-bellied beast
called Behemoth, burst loose the river weeds
in cloudy mud-mist down the stream; he feeds
grunting, suck-sucking Jordan with his feast
of grass; slow swings his low eyes to the east,
blinks as the sun strikes, turns away; he needs
no such clean light, shafting the trodden reeds;
logs it in water-holes till day has ceased.

Drowse and be comfortable; lie, Behemoth
under the cross-stick shadow, tremulous veil
heat-vibrant, quick in the slant-broken stems.
So has he made you; bone and sinew both
of iron, that his image man may quail
at sight of you, and clutch his garment's hems.

THE SPIRIT SHALL RETURN

Often the things I see are tired,
the sounds I hear lag halting back;
I lump the world along with me,
a body in a shouldered sack

    that huddles with its mortal weight
    the loaded wrist against my throat;
    the silence runs upon my soul,
    the dust has fingers on my coat.

The rising dust that pulls me down
knows well I walk the road alone,
or the road walks, where I might be
entombed, and straining at the stone.

Stars that lit Jacob's ladder once
drop out of heaven to the dust
or heaven itself is there, and there
the treasuries of moth and rust;

I lump the world along with me
though heaven is eaten, and the night
poured out upon the sea of glass
obliterates the Light of Light.

This way's the only narrow way,
swagging the body of this death,
to know this life, and that I live.
Dust unto dust, the preacher saith.

THE AGONY

Stammering wind this night
gustily utters
its deaf-mute cries
and the rain
trapped fingers tapping wakes me
under the windowless rock
outside this house.
There, there again!
Out there alone somebody sighed,
a scrabbling sigh of sharp unpartnered
pain:
        so dark,
dark in the heart, and still
the sighing wind, the rain
dropping, dropping,
the bloody sweat down-dropping,
oh God!
can pity be worth so much?

SCREENED

He dressed his love in a fine dress
praising its swing and suppleness:

they laughed to see the boy at play
and said, he had a pretty way;

and he dipped to a dainty kiss,
said, this my love, my love is this:

content they were to see the slow
meet of the flesh so lightly go—

good and his evil went their round
and shoulder-looking knowledge frowned.

HOST OF THE AIR

Out of the living pit
deep under the moon
beat to the fiend's tune
round the tall black-lit
scarp of the moon flame
they whom God gave no name.

Earth, water and fire
labour and breathe them out,
twist they a man with doubt
and a knife at his desire,
they are the piercingest
pain without a breast.

Who knows that he is known
by name to Christ his Lord,
his peace, his sword?
Each son of man alone
walks with a wind of wings
of the nameless things.

STATUS QUO

If these stuck clods were blasted wide
the rubble raked apart to give
the sun below, they'd spill their pride
and learn of worms the way to live.

THE SERPENT

The plague's about along the street.
In proud decay the dead go by
and, failing flesh on lagging feet,
move on the many marked to die:

there is no mourning day and night,
nor simple tears nor common sorrow,
since death today strikes at the sight
and reaches for the heart tomorrow;

so no-one sees the shrouded men
about their business through the day
dividing to their dust again,
for whom there is no other way,

for the one dust has nourished them
and thickened round their clodded feet;
so earth will earth at last condemn
to earth's last pitiable retreat.

Christ take the whip of knotted cord,
flay out the money-changing dead!
Christ bring the labourer's reward,
the burning thirst on Dives' head!

See where the healing serpent stands,
Christ lifted up — his felon's crown
crush on our heads, and set our hands
to turn the whole world upside down.

APOCALYPTIC

Yet a star will speak
and the swift wheels which spatter
bright hours with idle dirt
the wheels which whirl and hurt
will gasp off at the hub:
yet a star will speak.

The smoke of their burning
chokes the song of the day,
incense of quick decay,
still the wheels whining pray
God burn us up, burn up.
The smoke of their burning.

Man, blood in your head
flies thick with the spin of the rim
round with you bound and broken
while a star has not spoken.
Does it sparkle behind the ball,
man, blood in your head?

There is no loosing hands,
the hour is the power which moves,
the very pivot is space
in whose gift's no grace
for there is no tangent,
there is no loosing hands

till a star speak to a man
and two shall join to him
and the pain die in the burning
and the seized wheels cease turning:
guard our strength as we may,
till a star speak to a man.

POWER OF THE MANY

Against these eyes where is a man to hide?
Cover him close to friend with the worm inside,
cover him close by the intimate lips of the worm
where the bed is soft, for he hates anything firm.

The eyes have a hard way with a waking man
in their force, forcing sleep down the throat till he can
breathe his best in the mothering coil of the worm
where the bed is soft, for he hates anything firm.

'Fill his heart, Christ, that he wake and walk in sight
'of the cloud by day, the untouchable flame by night,
'so the withering eyes recoil from the wakened man
'heartened, hardened for heaven, so that he can
'straighten his way from the smothering loop of the worm
'where the bed is soft, for he hates anything firm'.

ON RELIEF

They gave your hands a grubbing-tool
and you have learnt to use the thing:
you thought, a man's a bloody fool
who starves when work is offering.

And there's a stiffness in your eyes
that is not earth nor bodily pain;
your eyes give nothing to the dust
though foot and hand shake out the chain:

this iron marks you man, bound low
under a mad king's blind control,
who wills you change, you would or no,
his mass-compassion for a soul.

THREE POEMS
1935

ASPECTS OF MONISM

i

This was untrue, that there is division
between body and mind, making sin
and matter for secret speaking or derision
out of an act where sight and strength begin:

this believing, I could not give you alone
body's touch and power, nor want of you
warm sense only, since these are known
but as form of thought, weapon of will to do.

So pity is born of power, love of subjection —
blood is swift to learn and the mind slow —
did I think before, would there be recollection
by the mind of error when it did not know?

Now it is too late to save the deceit;
it is death or whole acceptance of the vision
of beauty gone down full-eyed in defeat
earth receiving her. There is no division.

ii

Nothing passes, all is the one moment
possessing richly world's breadth; and the clear
succession, which is illusion, of jewelled hours
is a burning peace in the eyes of one woman;
and it is time there was an end of asking.

iii

In the dawning eye only has the sun its being,
waking to dawn in a man's body, burning
as ultimate knowledge looked fairly in the face;
and where lastly is the act of seeing?

And the day has one white foot on the very far
first step from darkness, and a white arm takes
the sea in a bowl held upward in a glory.
There is no earth nor any other star;

only, they have claimed arrogantly
that it is possible to see the sun
and the rising wonder and the burden of lightening
consciousness. How should they see

into the bodiless unity, scatter the strength
which is both sight of the eyes and utmost vision
from the first sun step to the end in darkness?
If any god has led us to this length

there is a temple to be overthrown
before any man can wake with the earth's waking
or answer the love which crosses the sea at morning
or visit the mountains and be known.

iv

So with me you must come into certain places
where the blood of earth runs clear
in a slim green plant and in a standing tree
and there are no separate death-hardened faces

dividing in a dream the shadow of a man;
then it may be life will look on life,
eye into eye and see no difference,
but earth, love, death, lost in a single span.

RESTRAINT

For pity of your own heart, think
of the way you would choose:
I shall tell you of its certain end
and what your heart may lose:

you may have at last slight memory
of seas crossed, other lands,
strange speech, strange faces
and the work of strange hands.

For a time your heart will plead with you
for space in which to see
the sun rise upon dark places
that were lost utterly;

but there will be silence in a while
and another memory
of a dream broken and beauty left
at the border of the sea:

there is one sun the world over
and the one heaven's blue;
and one heart risen with the morning
can light the world for you.

Many cities and new marvels
only blind the eyes
which a flower might have perfected
the hour before it dies:

never look long at a flower —
a moment, at the most —
for fear your heart walk desolate
in a cold land lost.

THE WILDERNESS

Soul, put on now as vesture
well-chosen word and gesture;
let good manners attend you
and common speech defend you:

the stars your enemies,
the tall malicious trees
and the sunlit flesh of her
who is life's doorkeeper

know where you will tread;
be cold then, as if dead,
and beauty may desert you
nor find where to hurt you.

ENEMIES
1937

NEW ZEALAND CITY

Small city, your streets
lack legend, lead nowhere
proud shrined, notorious
for a church or a brothel.

Your potentates cringe,
nobody notices.
Nations do not quote
your newspapers. London
has spawned. Here are banks
in the egg, Beaverbrook
foetuses, Chamberlain
foetuses, toy trains,
mud pies and sandpits,
an unstained sky.

Yet the cloud
curdles in the wind
pitted with blue
or the cloud returns
laden, still laden
after the rain

and many coats hang
from a hanger or shoulder
and pens by the thousand
scratch like rats' teeth
busy in the wall

and a rubbery squeal
tells the tarseal
that a man goes home
at evening which must follow
any toil's end.

Land of new hopes
with a thousand years'
despair, of children
with senile faces,
this land, these islands:
the shadow of Europe
falls, over the fallen
walls of an empire:
the planet called Asia
spins visibly
from here, small city,
to the naked eye
some worlds away
in the northern sky:
and eastward the white
hospital where
the sick breathe air
conditioned air
and dollar by dollar
the beads are told there.

Serf to them all
for pleasure or pain;
betrayed to the world's
garret and gutter,
sold for the export
price of butter.

RECALL TO EARTH

Together let us regain the earth's friendship.
The poplar spire topped by no cross
may be our temple tower, of delight in wind
or of roadside riches no loss.

Fear, iron-eyed chauffeur of ambition,
drives daily to the gold-lettered door
him whose property increases and multiplies,
like every private pontiff and public bore.

Monkey chatter in the newest manner
offends your spirit. Foolishness harries you.
Will you play bridge? Tongues fence, lips mince.
Trapped handshake, mechanical howdyadoo.

Shall we put up with it no longer than
body and soul can bear? Life gets to its feet, —
Excuse us, the wind is waiting, the unpaid sun
babysits for us in another street.

CHIEF END

Drag a star down to the office table —
what sort of light is that to work by?
Rising wind will confuse important papers
not contributing to efficiency.

Get up at daybreak, seek bed at dusk?
So little time there would be for pleasure.
We shall save money and buy a car
and cultivate a right use of leisure.

FACTORY AT NIGHT

This light both whip and burden to your eyes
that wince, being tender yet. After the glory
of wide-armed sun at morning, leaves warmed through,
the blood's green quickened, the day dies
not gratefully for you,
but a mocked day dawns on the plaster,
strokes of an idiot's brush;
oil streams, steel slides faster
and faster the shadows rush
under the whipping lights
overhead under and over again.

Fish out of water, these eyes,
and the net is pain.

COLONIAL OUTLOOK

Night, will not night identical draw down
merciful shutter on our unimportance
as (one imagines) mountainous dark will drown
organic millions in dreamy pretence
of works relaxed by deathly creeds, in sleep?

So many thousand fewer paved miles
so many fewer turns of shuddering tyres
so many fewer strong, remote smiles
(with us) shield rout of refugee desires;
insignificant conflict, late begun,
and comic disaster — surely bitterness
and fear have here as central impetus?

Our beds empty, streets a desert no less
than in the other provinces of the sun:
yet we remain, dog-at-heel, obsequious.

A WOMAN IN MIND

i

I have lit a single lamp
and laid my fire beneath
for cold faint-sun days
of frost and cloudy breath.

Her eyes my early lamp
in this winter of the heart;
her body, limbs burning,
holds bitterness apart.

Shadows prank my walls;
outside, rain is flying:
ere my light and my fire die
I too shall be dying.

ii

Your face between my hands
and your eyes open to me,
it is as if I stood
beside a great sea;
for nothing is so still
or perfect in its pride
or such deep semblance, as
the flesh I stand beside.

iii

My hands worship
you with suppliant touch
in whatever part seeking
to know you bodily.

Nothing is withheld
from us in our free
city of love, we conceal
not from any sense.

To shrink from flesh
is to offend the spirit —
who can divide them
one from the other?

Now you receive
hand at breast and thigh,
I suppliant; but soon
equal communion.

iv

As the green music compassing
all earth that listens in the spring
so is the semblance when your nearness
shakes taut and void to broken clearness
and music, music cries to be
about the way you walk to me.

v

Who am I
that I should own
so fair a field
and meet, for yield?

That in this earth's
deep, sweet warmth
my seed should stir
(the sun loves her)

drinking bright rain
in womb of tenderness,

god's gate, the same,
Mary without blame?

Since it is mine
this earth, her flesh,
bears that which I
wanting, should die.

vi

By pain outspoken
a precious thing is broken,
peace destroyed by pain
no words can bring again.

May sun never bless me
and loud winds oppress me
if from me is heard
a destructive word.

Shut my mouth upon your breast;
now I have confessed,
on my lips let move
breath only of love.

vii

In the time of your conceiving
which shall be in spring
we shall die with flowers, together
in all our blossoming.

A rose shall ask your lips
close, as never before
when summer has deepened
and life is at the door.

Autumn shall bring us then
leaves' grace in falling,
wind-lightened, lost suns
without pain recalling.

Winter, not an enemy
to earth's true lover,
but womb of new sowing,
shall cover us over.

MOUNTAIN ELEGY

i

Immaculate wing unfolding slowly enfolding
white light, sun wakening the great bird roosted
on the broken edges of a thousand feet.
Portent of flight till mountain dawn withholding.

Nightlong dreamless motionless among intermittent
huge migrations of wind, loud hosts in passing
leaving louder silences, bird upon the cliff
knows morning in each cell, light palpitant.

Morning has no audible herald at this height:
all is translated, song into flight;
trumpet note into arrogance of light
bannered fiercely through the passes,
as striking fire from new-split gem
leaps at the haggard eastward masses
cracking gold from the heart of them.

ii

Voiceless but the only articulate
motion on earth's frozen lip,
beautiful for invisible mate
the wing trembles to the tip;

if dumb space did not intervene
drowning familiarities,
could be heard lightly the dark lean
claws finding grip to rise.

Ascending cry across the blue.
Upward the wing'd glory breaks
and suddenly morning is in view
which is not till the creature wakes.

iii

The eye is now withdrawn, extreme reach of self
and extreme sacrifice, in rhythmic reasonless flying;
nothing heard or seen, everything heard and seen,
that topmost life realised once in dying.

Life has crept above the broken edges, has leapt
assured into remote clasp of snow and sun
which after all live but by living blood, waiting
on the reviving wing for their day begun.

iv

Smears of a dark hand,
piecemeal evening
swarms from lower land
to the breach hasting,
shuddering wings
forget high-noon fire,
on low crag at rest
searching no higher.

Sapphire clouded
white garment torn
young body shrouded
bright hair shorn.

Slowly
        enfolding light
only articulate
              nightlong
                          dreamless.

Death is most in mind
in this mountain evening without wind.

ENEMIES

Detestable gutter child, if you knew
how we hate you, I and my kind,
you would scramble bawling with terror
to that refuge behind
the sodden stinking privy at the back
of the two rooms stuck by the railway track.

SLUM

Walking in the garden of our Father
I find evil places; it is rather
as if honouring death we
had planted here Gethsemane.

Though Christ came from God, he
taught us the love of death and agony.

The garden wall is iron, its soil
is dust choking those who toil;
boards rot in the shadow, some few
are aware of a heart rotting too.

Christ loved mankind it is true,
but said 'the poor you have always with you.'

Almsgiving knows no pity;
charity collected in the city
is self-defence of deep hate
bribing the enemy from the gate.

As Christ taught we feed our enemies
fearing the unblunted enmities.

Between the factory and
the filthy house I stand
a moment, seeing a woman sitting
glance at me over her knitting;

better forget sixpenny charity
when the poor carry their hate honestly.

We have agents behind the lines,
peddlers of promise, seers of signs,
preaching that the starving should not covet
good things, bringing Moses' law to prove it:

yet Moses' case is scarcely comparable
with these who have no manna for the table.

Walking in the garden one sees
so many of our enemies,
hearts fix'd strength undecay'd,
that I wonder that we are not afraid:

but we are safe until the day
our weapons show obvious decay.

REMAINDER

I go home with my wife
and we talk about you
who go home with your wives,
possibly mentioning us.

We all went into the sea
muddy soup stirred not
only by feet but wind
also, long ladle of ocean.

Up again Aphrodite
neat in wool and rubber;
lumps out of the soup;
shake off the drips.

Such is our contact;
faith our mainstay, you
possibly mentioning us.

ORBIT

With so great wonder, at times fear,
I hear and see the distraught people
in twitching panic tread the collapsed hours
(time's rhythm wrench'd, rush'd with pale speed,
time in time machine-maddened): I must keep
heart's beat by you who follow the sun
whose blood keeps time of the sun the governor;
spite of chaos' steam and steel writhing
heart learns of you right motion,
season's swing, curve of rejoicing comet,
remote, holy obedience of the stars.

THE LEAVES DEAD

Drained flesh and hardened
by winter wind and water
leaves fill, with poison
part of their own nature;

blown from safe mooring
above heavy water
up heaven's wind-tunnel,
leaves fill the chamber
of sight, with death-yellow
spume lightly hardened.

Mud, leaf-rot, water
mix under a tree,
dissolution found in them
part of their own nature.

PAID WELL

No more burns the fire within the word.
Use stiffens the rhythm, effaces the image
which came and went like flame.

Great waters
are come upon the world, all cold
untroubled by birth and death alike.

NOT IN NARROW SEAS
1939

DEDICATION

To him who can distinguish
In an unfeigned anguish
What is general
From what is personal,
Who has heard optimism
Crash in the last chasm
And knows hope more near
His heart's despair.

Towards mid-day, on December 13, in the year 1642 — the year of English revolution, of the death of Galileo, and the birth of Newton — the eyes of a sailor, straining over the waters of the Pacific, saw about 60 miles to the eastward 'a great land uplifted high' . . .

. . . The Dutch christened the shore thus uncertainly glimpsed New Zealand . . .

. . . Canterbury (was settled) by J. R. Godley (later of the War Office) and an Episcopalian pilgrimage in 1850. For some years these provinces were proudly conscious of their nationality and their virtue; the obliterating passage of time, alas! has merged them with their fellows in a common mediocrity . . .

. . . Yet in the midst of converging cables, shipping and wireless communication, it has remained always isolated; and in that verdant isolation perhaps lies the remote secret — if there is one — of the national life . . . and it may be that in the 20th century the making of new nationalities is an anachronism, as it certainly is a danger.

J. C. BEAGLEHOLE   *New Zealand: A Short History* (1936)

STATEMENT

In your atlas two islands not in narrow seas
Like a child's kite anchored in the indifferent blue,
Two islands pointing from the Pole, upward
From the Ross Sea and the tall havenless ice:
Small trade and no triumph, men of strength
Proved at football and in wars not their own:

So much and the soft weather you may call your own
And the week-end bach by the salt healing seas,
Deep soil and shingle-slide to try your strength
Under the sun or dark-to-thunder blue;
Under your impudent feet the glacier's ice
Stirs like the hour-hand as you stumble upward.

In the little city's scattered smoke look upward
Feeling the various active fields your own
And your terrible equity in the blazing ice:
Forgetting the bondholder over the seas
And the foreigner's far cry, his bending blue,
And fear in a fast car finding its own strength.

Look upward. Now comes near a test of strength,
You at the desk and in the street look upward,
Both the county chairman and the airman in blue,
Take courage for these also are your own:
The pay envelope and the letter overseas,
Shame at night and ambition thatis like ice.

The girls' feet crackle on the pavement ice,
A little warfare with superior strength,
To the Office. Enemies have crossed the seas
And hold the passes that enfold you upward,
Over Cook's peak and the lakes still your own
The aircraft crawling in the ill-mapped blue:

Not in a life your triumph nor the blue
Empty of fear, from the high chasmed ice
To the sheep lands, cattle lands that are your own:
Inheritors of an unrejoicing strength,
Driving, driven to market, heaving upward
A dust, your landfall's cloud mark and the sea's:

Therefore I sing your agonies, not upward,
For the two islands not in narrow seas
Cringe in a wind from the world's nether ice.

I

In a little artificial port with five jetties, overseas shipping waits to be loaded with the primary products from which the Dominion derives its wealth. This is a natural point from which to begin a study of the birth, life and growth of a nation now nearly 100 years old. Attempts are being made to establish a culture similar to that which Europe has taken 1,000 years to build; but the real ambitions of this people are naive enough — 'a radio, perhaps a car.'

    The water is burred with rain.
    Men scrape rough iron, squatting
    On the slung plank, setting
    Knee and toe to the ship's flank.

    Rust and dust and the keen
    Wind strapping the ankle;
    Chips from the chisels sprinkle
    Down to the blue mud.

    There are five wharves.
    To-day the port is quite full.
    They will load mutton and wool
    As soon as the rain stops.

    The Minister believes
    The price is sufficient to cover
    Labour costs and something over
    For a radio, perhaps a car.

II

At the time of writing it is more than 80 years since the Canterbury Province of New Zealand was settled. There arrived in the port (then not equipped for the handling of mutton carcases) in 1850, four sailing vessels, bearing the persons, livestock and other goods of the settlers. From the shore of the harbour, a seven-miles gulf of ancient volcanic formation, they climbed to the hilltop and looked out over 100 miles of plain: a country they were to conquer without force or danger.

    Eighty years since salted sails
    Dropped among these hills
    And the iron water closed on
    The anchor's dry iron.

    Bedding and tents and stores
    Littered the frontiers
    Of a country taken
    To be stripped and broken.

    Not leap of capture theirs,
    But as who safely dares,
    Seizing without sword
    Front garden and backyard.

III

For many months they had been at sea. It was a pilgrimage under the blessing of the Church of England, more definitely religious in its professions, perhaps, than any since the Mayflower.

Strut on the beach loos'd nervous limbs
And they praised God with bad hymns,
Quavering in a huge volcanic crack
With the iron water at their back.

Doubtless their liturgy had prayer
For establishing truth and virtue there,
For the wind clipping the reverent scalps
Howled the joke to the high Alps:

'We shall not blacken this land O Lord,
Thou hast given us without sword;
Our weapon and our lust lie at home
And in peace for peace we are come.'

IV

Apparently there was a chance here for a clean break. The dark places of industrial England, its poverty and diseases, were left behind. Only the best had been taken, it seemed, of the English tradition. The liturgy of the Church of England, immigrants of picked stock, sufficient capital to provide for material needs and their development.

        Escape in seeming from smoke and iron,
        The hammered street and the hot wheels,
        Clanging conquest of the deep-rich hills.

        Left behind the known germ and poison
        Breeding and soaking in decrepit soils.

        Jerusalem is built as a city
        That is at unity in itself,
        Built with liturgy and adequate capital
        Dwelling of the elect, the selected immigrants.

V

Iron, first introduced to the islands when the ships dropped anchor off shore, soon becomes more firmly established. It must be noted that the traditional courage of pioneers becomes, in social terms, merely the furious sorties of man confronted with the unknown. Frustration drives men to seek a new country; but the savagery of the new land threatens an even more terrible frustration; so that fear swallows creative effort; and the sole effective desire remaining is to conserve and extend the illusion of life in the old world. So the cycle is completed in time, and the original frustration is perpetuated.

Blood in the climbing limb
No fear checking the pulse,
Pulls mountains down flat,
Erects cathedrals.

The superior race, Lo!
The pass in a twinkling
Yields the advancing column
A top-gear incline.

Green grows the bungalow
At the courageous heels,
Valour makes home for fear
Under hesitant sails:

A beginning, a beginning
A fresh start in life
With a blue-new shovel
And a rusted belief.

Iron for axe and hammer
Iron for rod and nail
Iron for the door-knocker
Like the head of a bull.

Where the first anchor's cable
Slackened into sleep
Iron threads rock for prison
Bars on the harbour slope.

VI

The Church is quick to follow the imperial lead. Shrewdly, she acquires property, and ownership is thus sanctified. The Gospel, it might be imagined, would seek to find realisation in the building of a new social order. But the Church is chiefly concerned with re-establishing and conserving an order in which she has learnt to flourish. Any departure from that order is disquieting to her. It has been noticed that religion thrives best among the poor in spirit and in body.

>The bishop boundary-rides his diocese
>Carrying the sacraments at saddle-bow;
>The church equestrian christens peak and river
>Where land is cheap and the reapers are few.
>
>Years after where his lordship braved the ford
>Less hardy saints cross bridges in a gig:
>Good rents assure their stipends, not even
>Judas so providently kept the bag.
>
>A faith worthy of empire; ere the four
>Earliest migrant vessels put to sea
>The wise company granted God permission
>To work His passage to the colony.
>
>Certified seed in a prepared soil—
>What land would not give the approved return?
>Here's no renewal of the world's youth,
>But age-soured infancy, a darkened dawn.

VII

The pleasant work of exploring and building proceeds, making the country fit for civilised people to live in.

Woman who wakes beneath casewood and canvas
Salutes sunrise excellently painted,
Warm familiar among unfamiliar
To which heart unwilling consented.

Waking next morning, moving curtain, she
Sees front plot fenced, path in place;
The cloud, the mountain-terror tamed now
Framed to taste for parlour chimneypiece.

Not lessened the offensive against fear,
Eye cracking distance, foot on ford and steep;
Each to his tools his trade and his journey,
Restoring reason, the known scene and shape.

VIII

For the young child a different destiny is expected. His surroundings are clean, hardly-broken country. For that reason it is assumed that he has a rich, unassessed heritage. In fact, as time has demonstrated, his heritage is already bought and sold at market price. If there is any gain it is not here. Even those to whom they are politically sacred admit that ownership and trade have brought their inevitable attendant evils. These are more potent here, where there are fewer escapes by culture or tradition from the economic cycle of strength, work and food.

Child of the stolen country
Tumbling on the raw clay,
By the fence of green wood
Given to play

With terrible idle earth,
Mountains and two seas
Opposing with patience
Endless enmities—

Child, old evil sprouts
Along the new track
From home's front door
To privy at the back
And where scrub is cleared
Round the neighbour's shack.

Not your destiny nor
This land's your shaping:
The sowing yours
Another's the reaping.

(The seed itself tainted
In the excited soil,
Yellow the trampled ford
Where the floods boil.)

Cancel the vision and
Wipe prayer from lip:
God comes not to market
Nor saints by ship.

IX

In a brief conversation the Teacher explains to the Pupil the meaning of empire. God and the flag are one, national pride being (by naive admission) the solution of all social opposites and discrepancies. Only the wind serves still to remind the patriot that the fight for liberty continues, the pupil apparently convinced by Authority, is still somewhat corrupted by the wind. The wind, it will be observed, has the last word.

Teacher: Haul the flag to the top of the mast,
Let it break there proclaiming brightly
The imperial message for this is the day
For remembering the nation our creator:
Honour the motherland as privilege and duty.

Pupil: See how the deep gusts out of the mountain
Snatch at the flag as if they hated it.

Teacher: Do not speak of hatred of the flag.
It has God's cross, see, in the white and red.

Pupil: It is a sinful wind that does not love
The flag that bears God's cross.
Eighty years ago this flag was brought
To struggle upon this pole to-day
Over a million heads microcosm
Of the nation which colonised these islands;
A greatness not to be straitened,
Not by wind and ocean beaten off.

Teacher: That is to-day's lesson, Move on, please
And see the convenient state prepared for you
From the field the mountain and the shingly river.
Walk by the sundial in the front garden,
The double garage, the gravelled backyard.

Pupil: The flag flies high over that large building,
Four floors glassed and terraced, idle lawns:
I suppose that is the Governor's residence?

Teacher: That is the mental hospital where 5,000
Live, poor loonies, getting the best treatment.

Pupil: God's cross over the kingdom of the mad.
The mad are a great nation to extend
Their empire to the islands of the sea.

Teacher: The wind blew out their brains. We take the tram
(A municipal enterprise of some importance)
To another quarter of the growing city,
The bungalows in rows smartly painted
And the educated citizen returning
After work with a friend to make four at bridge.
Tourists have declared that the standard of living
Is higher than anywhere in Europe.

Pupil: Two rooms lift rusted iron, a kennel roof
By the fleshy brick of the twine factory.
This, I take it, the penal settlement.

Teacher: One of the poorer suburbs, the colony
Of those who heard the wind, the enemy:
Such refuse heaps make disposal a problem
But the contractors it is said are doing well.

Pupil: God's cross over the kingdom of the poor.

The Wind: The flag rides rattling at the hoist
At prison and at madhouse door;
I swell'd their sails and what's the end?
The poor insane and the insane poor.

X

    The new country must be aware of the dangerous extent to which it is only a flattery by imitation of the old. Being a flattery it tends to imitate in the grosser respects only. The street scene, the cheap entertainment, are all faithfully reproduced. The values whose death is celebrated everywhere under buildings of iron and concrete, are no more apparent here than in the old countries. There is reproduction, but not resurrection.

>Jaunty hopes that play
>Against the cynical scene:
>New land New Zealand
>Dancing before the throne.
>
>Now while the gilt is fresh
>In our intimate theatre,
>Listen and you will hear
>The old, old gags recur:
>
>Apprenticed to this stage
>We thumb the greasy script:
>Here we foreknow laughter,
>There we shall have wept.
>
>Who tinkers with the lines?
>It makes no difference:
>The old play that catches
>Nobody's conscience.
>
>Reproduction, reproduction
>Of the curved, the angled, the tangible
>Street measurable block by block:
>
>Never resurrection
>Of entombed pity, only discernible
>Vanity of the practised trick.

Sensitive the film senselessly
Unrolls the death-embracing images:
Island and ocean a theatre

Screening a weary self-flattery
Where colour and where courage is
Costumed secondhand, in character.

XI

Having matched itself against the rest of the world in a game at which the rest of the world is by experience superior, the infant nation suffers an increase of frustration. Therefore it assumes a proprietary pride in the natural phenomena of the country. These, as well as the fruits of the soil, must be sold, to enable the nation to continue living just a little beyond its means. Foreign films and motor-cars (without which life is obviously intolerable) must be paid for. Mountains and other pleasant places must be, if necessary, blasted with facilities to satisfy the scenery-swallowing appetites of wealthy visitors from abroad. With such assets and others, the Government may borrow abroad to provide increasing facilities for civilised comfort: generally speaking, no other interpretation of civilisation is commonly admitted.

  Naked goes the land
  Under the sweating hand
  Of the lover of a night,
  While the procuress
  Has eyes on a dress
  Of innocent white.

  You are on a holiday trip, sir,
  And what do you think of our country?
  Let us discuss beauty
  And various scenic attractions:
  Tell me our alps excel
  Switzerland and the Rockies.

  Interviewed by 'The Blast'
  Sir Bradford classed
  Our mountain scenery
  With Switzerland's best
  Was deeply impressed
  Is at present the guest
  Of Dean Horn at the Deanery.

  (O lord, O lord, lord, O lord
  Make them say the encouraging word)

The young athletes ran
Nowhere at the Games,
No sporting year-book
Lists their names;
Overseas visitors
Are nevertheless polite:
They arrive in the morning
And leave at night.

Spirit, O spirit of the first-comers under sail
Where lost, you spirit?
                              Under a movie-theatre seat
Later disposed of by the police at auction.
However, there is ample pleasant distraction
Many arts of frustration to emulate
At $3\frac{1}{2}$ per cent. on a borrowed smile.

XII

Yet, out of the orgy of imitation, there will in time be born men of spirit. So far the country has not been able to contain its great spirits; that, perhaps, is because there have been none great enough to expand the country till it is able to sustain them. Poets, painters, musicians, scientists will suffer agonies in a country serving under gross masters. But out of their sufferings the wheat lands, the cattle country and the sheep country, may be born again. At present, however, an artist can only suffer, and record his suffering; hoping to make others suffer with him the necessary pains of first self-knowledge.

>Where Van Gogh struck his seed
>Flat France twirled with pain:
>To these Pacific boulders
>There will come men
>
>Put to such planting
>After the rusted harrow
>Mining among mountains
>With their seed of sorrow:
>
>The vertical ice, the dry
>Shriek of the kea
>A howl of misery like
>The cornfields of Auvers.

EPILOGUE

Bring me an axe and spade:
For this is insolent country,
James Cook's pig-farm
Without rule or road.

Bring me a winding-sheet:
For the brown singing people
Affront with death our triumph, an
Unangry death without fight.

When I my grave have made
I shall write to friends at Home,
And with an English accent
How shall I be afraid?

Let winds and tempests beat
On 1,000 bungalows,
To our sad suburban funeral
Drag followers on foot.

Down I'll lie
As cold as clay
Thank God *true love*
doth pass away,

The empire and the empty lands
The iron and the golden sands
Dredged and dumped
With the wheezing sea clay.

ISLAND AND TIME
1941

... The air of their islands is mainly fresh from the sea, and the rainfall abundant from the mountains whereon it condenses, from which, in some places, a violent sirocco results. Their present condition depends on the state of peoples a great distance off, and their communications with these. As yet they have no future of their own; and when at length one confronts them, they shall awake to find where they lie, and what realm it was they so rudely and rashly disturbed.

D'ARCY CRESSWELL Present Without Leave

SENTENCE

Tentative the houses
Unhaunted over tombs;
Wind shakes the standing
Timber, shakes rooms
Where cold under rimu
Rafters they discover
The wind wet with change, and
The stranger for lover.

THE UNHISTORIC STORY

Whaling for continents coveted deep in the south
The Dutchman envied the unknown, drew bold
Images of market-place, populous river-mouth,
The Land of Beach ignorant of the value of gold:
    Morning in Murderers' Bay,
    Blood drifted away.
    It was something different, something
    Nobody counted on.

Spider, clever and fragile, Cook showed how
To spring a trap for islands, turning from planets
His measuring mission, showed what the musket could do
Made his Christmas goose of the wild gannets.
    Still as the collier steered
    No continent appeared;
    It was something different, something
    Nobody counted on.

The roving tentacles touched, rested, clutched
Substantial earth, that is, accustomed haven
For the hungry whaler. Some inland, some hutched
Rudely in bays, the shaggy foreshore shaven,
    Lusted, preached as they knew;
    But as the children grew
    It was something different, something
    Nobody counted on.

Green slashed with flags, pipeclay and boots in the bush,
Christ in canoes and the musketed Maori boast;
All a rubble-rattle at Time's glacial push:
Vogel and Seddon howling empire from an empty coast
    A vast ocean laughter
    Echoed unheard, and after
    All it was different, something
    Nobody counted on.

The pilgrim dream pricked by a cold dawn died
Among the chemical farmers, the fresh towns; among
Miners, not husbandmen, who piercing the side
Let the land's life, found like all who had so long
    Bloodily or tenderly striven
    To rearrange the given,
    It was something different, something
    Nobody counted on.

After all re-ordering of old elements
Time trips up all but the humblest of heart
Stumbling after the fire, not in the smoke of events;
For many are called, but many are left at the start,
    And whatever islands may be
    Under or over the sea,
    It is something different, something
    Nobody counted on.

THE DANCE

If music may save
Then dance to what you have,
To the wind in the angle
Of an old tin shed
To the whistling of a river
To the creaking of a bed
To the rattle of shingle
To the whisper of sand
To the tractor in the paddock
To a mouth-organ band.
> *Over the bones of an ear*
> *Goes wind, goes fear.*

Will you come, curse
You? Nothing could be worse
Than standing drumming
While the dancers disperse
Than a turf unbroken
Than roses in a row
Than an old man reading
Than a new radio
Than a long itching finger
Than nothing left to know.
> *Over the bones of an ear*
> *Goes wind, goes fear.*

FANTASY ON A HILLSIDE

Sun's hammer swinging at the skull
Starts a lark singing off the hill,
Pacific stoops a broad blue back
Lower, the higher loops the track;
    Eyes brim, tilt,
    More sea is spilt
Over the rolling convex floor
Between the sky-sill and the shore.

Marooned I gaze, marooned I climb,
Pouring seas to bottomless Time
Whose vaporous chasm will not float
Knotted raft or hollowed boat:
    Horizon's brink
    Should stretch, I think,
With height, and I, with strides immense,
Climb easily into continents.

TIME

I am the nor'west air nosing among the pines
I am the water-race and the rust on railway lines
I am the mileage recorded on the yellow signs.

I am dust, I am distance, I am lupins back of the beach
I am the sums the sole-charge teachers teach
I am cows called to milking and the magpie's screech.

I am nine o'clock in the morning when the office is clean
I am the slap of the belting and the smell of the machine
I am the place in the park where the lovers were seen.

I am recurrent music the children hear
I am level noises in the remembering ear
I am the sawmill and the passionate second gear.

I, Time, am all these, yet these exist
Among my mountainous fabrics like a mist,
So do they the measurable world resist.

I, Time, call down, condense, confer
On the willing memory the shapes these were:
I, more than your conscious carrier,

Am island, am sea, am father, farm, and friend,
Though I am here all things my coming attend;
I am, you have heard it, the Beginning and the End.

DRY WEATHER

Like dry grass burning, nerves
Flicker and spring in my skull;
Now Plato burns, now the sea,
Now lips, now leaves, now all.
Not too close, lest pain
Make tinder of the flesh,
I run behind the running smoke
On the cold soft ash.

ST THOMAS'S RUINS

Bishop George Selwyn grew tired of wood;
Like Solomon he desired permanent materials,
Home comforts for his traveller God,
Cypress and spire, background for burials.

So rock hardly cool from the crater
Assumed devout posture; column and arch
Housed the Lord fittingly and to the better
Credit of His bride the Church.

But ocean weather sucked the ill-mixed mortar
In as many years as the Norman's nave
Had centuries falling; sand, faith's deserter,
Made paste for rain to grind his groove.

Ubi episcopus, ibi ecclesia. The storm
Outgunned in grace the Bishop's praying,
Blew to his knees the seed of this cabbage-palm
Whose tufted rood transfixes the toy ruin.

TIME AND THE CHILD

The Child: Now that I am born, Sir, I suppose
              You intend to put me to some use;
              You who have given both the place and the hour
              Give also some peculiar power
              And how best to employ it.

Time: To live and die.
              This warm sun will make the minutes fly.

The Child: I like the sound of that. But I am told
              That when your own fingers, Sir, have rolled
              This earth round once, the sun removes his face
              To other children in another place.
              What have you for me to do when that deep
              Shadow sits in the window?

Time: Why then, sleep,
              A trick of mine that makes the minutes go
              Faster than light in darkness.

The Child: I want to know
              What life and sleep are like. I saw my own face
              Yesterday in a mirror, it stood in space
              As separate as the sun.

Time: That is an illusion
              That can cause nothing but confusion.
              Has no-one told you it is a dangerous thing
              To imagine a shadow is continuing
              In any place?

The Child: Sir, there are people here
              Who go about so solid and so clear,
              So like a picture painted with wind and fire,
              You will not be impatient if I inquire
              If life and sleep are beautiful like these?

Time: No more than sand, mountainsides, and trees.

The Child: But they look different.

Time: They live and die.
With the warm sun I make the minutes fly.
Wind and fire vanish and blood runs dry.
I am sorry.

The Child: Then there is nothing else
Except those various minutes that like bells
Dissolve stroke into stroke. Sir, that must be true.
But what about these walls, this window too
Where the river lies along our iron fence
And mountains swim in the river. Is it sense
That these do not continue?

Time: All pretence.
Do you know that there are a thousand such
Rivers, and can your river matter much?
If you would see which way the minutes dance
There are rivers more significant in France
Than ever ditched this yellow island clay.
I speak of events and do not try to deceive.

The Child: Sir, that is more than I can ever believe.

Time: It is not required. Island and continent
Roll in the sun through the minute and the event;
Man, his hour, his marvellous thought descend
Through perpetual beginning and perpetual end.
Boy, if you can make that teaching known
You shall have a house stronger than stone,
You shall have the Danube and the Mexique Bay
And all the secular fury of Europe as well.

The Child: And what comes after that, Sir?

Time: Time will tell.

SONG

A bridge and a bronze creek
And below that a lake
And below that a swamp
And a smoking camp
Where man and his iron bathe
In the sweat of the earth

And above that the feet
Of the forest, the weight
Of the living towers,
And above that the powers
That turn the sun and the weak
Rocks with heat shake,

And between hanging
An invisible bird singing
Between the roof and the root
Lightly lips his flute;
Between the womb and the seed
The song is made:

'Who would live here
Let him be all fire,
Let him not flinch
From the shuddering slim branch,
Let him dare all alone
The direct sun;

'On the rock beneath
There goes death,
Iron in his hand
And his path planned,
Who heaps high the load
And plies the goad:

'Who would sing, the sea
Is his enemy,
Better die than be cursed
With that harsh thirst
By which the throat is wrung
Too dry for song.'

POLAR OUTLOOK

They arctic we antarctic;
Colder the southern cap, emptier the seas;
Horizon more emphatic
Stamps out one by one our flickering days.

Immature form, no nerves
Twangling a meaningful music; stimulus
Stops at a full gut; waves
Cast up such creatures when the southerlies pass.

No loving analysis of country,
Mountain or basin split, named, beautified,
Or noble house that a century
Stained with better than lamb's or rabbit's blood:

Tour us, tour us with funnels
Yellow and scarlet marching up the mist-
Filled lank-fronded channels;
By a prince's, by a peer's name we shall be blessed.

HOUSE AND LAND

Wasn't this the site, asked the historian,
Of the original homestead?
Couldn't tell you, said the cowman;
I just live here, he said,
Working for old Miss Wilson
Since the old man's been dead.

Moping under the bluegums
The dog trailed his chain
From the privy as far as the fowlhouse
And back to the privy again,
Feeling the stagnant afternoon
Quicken with the smell of rain.

There sat old Miss Wilson,
With her pictures on the wall,
The baronet uncle, mother's side,
And one she called The Hall;
Taking tea from a silver pot
For fear the house might fall.

People in the *colonies*, she said,
Can't quite understand . . .
Why, from Waiau to the mountains
It was all father's land.

She's all of eighty said the cowman,
Down at the milking-shed.
I'm leaving here next winter.
Too bloody quiet, he said.

The spirit of exile, wrote the historian,
Is strong in the people still.

He reminds me rather, said Miss Wilson,
Of Harriet's youngest, Will.

The cowman, home from the shed, went drinking
With the rabbiter home from the hill.

The sensitive nor'west afternoon
Collapsed, and the rain came;
The dog crept into his barrel
Looking lost and lame.
But you can't attribute to either
Awareness of what great gloom
Stands in a land of settlers
With never a soul at home.

THE SCENE

Bush falls like waves, there is little you can hear
    But the stumbling flight of pigeons
And the buried anger of a truck's first gear
Pounding in gorges the heat-massive day.
Here among shaggy mountains cast away
    Man's shape must be recast;
    Whatever he imagines
Here on the unpeopled diffident scene between
Tasman's great stones, Pacific's gradual sand;
    Whatever is possessed
Between borders of blackened punga, beyond the town
Where tarred roads into the scrub run blind.

On hills above harbours the old habit of cities
    Persists, as the exile unpacks
Small necessaries on nameless island jetties.
Hands reach north for warmth, out of the south
Come storm and silence like a blow on the mouth;
    Inland the remote passes
    By which Time protracts
Forms of failure, instruments of collapse,
Bare will the measure of all, iron at the heart,
    The unmoved moving faces
In streets gliding like the riding lights of ships
Ill-found, reef-destined even as they depart.

Sheep jostle under a loitering pillar of dust
    Ignorant of the course set
Over the hazy plain to the ultimate coast
And the tossed carcase, and still the drover knows
What township will be reached at the day's close;
    Time's principals decide
    How and where shall be met
Down by the viscid sea the high prosperous hulls
History sends hither for a spendthrift gesture:
    Ever the returning tide

May bear no ships, a sickening shriek of gulls
And the rabbit's tooth free of the steep pasture.

But festive on sale day come farmers driving
    With the great gold-haired pigs
And tottering calves in trailers, early arriving
At favoured hotels, merchants' and agents' doors;
Sons are photographed, leaving for the wars,
    And these maintain the price.
    Here will be one who begs
One season more to bind his difficult acres
Devoured by rivers or blind with early snow;
    Man's still equivocal face
Brave in cloudbursts, disordered by figures
When clerks confirm what the winds overthrow.

Measurement of mountains, measurement of waters,
    Power pulled from the lake,
Where never trod centaur nor strolled satyrs
Creating and mocking man's measureless shape.
Who mustering up creeks saw the lion leap?
    Who in the riverbed
    Saw earth open and shake?
Such instants hover at the fringes of trade
As ships swim and aircraft out of Time like birds;
    Passion, pity, and dread
Consigned south out of Time, for islanders made
Whom the world's waste so royally rewards.

Build then, build by the too roomy sea
    For conference with Time
Who kicks down hovels but loves ceremony
And, seeing some piteous splendour here, may land
Bringing gifts, the beginning and the end,
    That is, all man's desire
    That ever learned to dream.
Some day thought will startle the bush like scarlet,

The pillar of dust stand in the road a spinning
    Stiff legendary fire,
Ships come spanking home and passion make solid
Man's shape again with the end and the beginning.

MORNING MOON

There goes the morning moon
Dawn-dull, fire's day-colour,
Bleeding her light away again
As the night's compassion,
Slipping from breast and brain,
Leaves the dry waking pallor.

EXPECT NO SETTLEMENTS

Expect no settlements or certainties
From volleys in deserts, explosions by rivers;
By no such loud and bloody exorcism
Will thunder quit the hills, sourness the plain;
Now hopes go little beyond remission of taxes
Dangerous are tongues that wag of the desperate coast
To which all bear their obsolete equipment.

I have emplaced cannon at all my windows,
At midnight sharpened arrows with a carpenter's file,
By digging under a pear-tree found poor shelter;
Do you think there is energy unspent in battle?
No place I visit but has twist or scar of violence,
Though here's no war gear, regimental number,
Or picking over of the dead for burial.

Now that events zoom on with throttle wide,
Permitting one passage where a million clamour,
Now fronts dissolve and pestilence burns clear
Its lines of access to the spirit within,
Banish from this house the current fury;
Anticipate ruin, blank reversal of prayer;
Part death from doom, making it possible.

CRASH AT LEITHFIELD

Mischievous earth and sky were at their worst
That summer's day when they worried him to death
Down off his clattering biplane perch, the first
Last flutter of his only wings and his brief breath.

Low he flew, inexpert nerve straining,
Lens-curved Pegasus Bay—more Icarus he
Raw to wings made trial of his training
Thirty miles on the white seam of land and sea.

Leithfield and lupins, lower, till the roar
Lay flat as a tractor on the brackish land,
Stiffly gasping at each gust of the nor'
Wester. Imminence of engine's sound

Started eyes darting up in township and farm;
Suddenly machine turned man between earth and sun,
Struggling in sucking airs. Could ignorant alarm
Read in his wingtips what was urgent to be done?

Lower, like bird in wave-trough, gustily rearing
Inland, wing flashed sunnily; steep and slow
His wild pilotage had the farm women fearing
What faith in their darling's daring might undergo.

Did he know before they knew the instant had passed
When a touch might start the capable smooth climb?
Did he know which deafening second was the last?
Was there pause in purpose, then the downthrust of Time?

Steadily, gaily tilted to the sun, droning
Still under power, engine and gale together,
To naively cruel earth too swift declining,
To the haystack's and the gum-tree's windy weather;

And the crash, how gentle it was, how cool the cloud
Black-billowing like loam, and silent—
Ah, silence queerer than all—how small, not loud
When this was, we thought, to have been so violent.

And they were still sitting in the aeroplane
Said the baker's driver who sped to be in at the kill,
While it was burning; he said again and again
Both of them were sitting, they are sitting there still.

Some took home bits of scorched fabric and some
Said they thought he was trying to land, and all that day
We watched or heard aircraft after aircraft come
Like foul birds over the dead, and none to drive them away.

QUICK ONE IN SUMMER

Glass handle mugs the barman polishes
And his eye, his amber eye,
Swims in the dusty gulf with flies
Whose sun is skylights high
Slammed by the Pacific-lurching gale;
That timeless sea clocks in,
Rolling safe-conduited for those
Whose hour is closing-time.

Here they come who lean and laugh
Tranced by a dirty glass,
All in that strange sea-dimension
Where Time and Island cross.
What if the weather is hot and wild
And walls creak in the wind?
Sweat has its salt as well as the sea,
Blood runs away like sand.

LAKE MAPOURIKA

The lake's a merry bitch.
She smiles at everyone
With an eye like fire and needles;
Her buoyant breast the sun
Paws and pets, and her secrets
Where young men dive and spill
Their heat in weedy water's
Dark unremorseful chill.

COUNTRY SCHOOL

North Canterbury

You know the school; you call it old—
Scrub-worn floors and paint all peeled
On barge-board, weatherboard, and gibbet belfry.

Pinus betrays, with rank tufts topping
The roof-ridge, scattering bravely
Nor'west gale as a reef its waves
While little girls squeal at skipping
And magpies hoot from the eaves:

For scantling Pinus stands mature
In less than the life of a man;
The rusty saplings, the school, and you
Together your lives began.

O sweet antiquity! Look, the stone
That skinned your knees. How small
Are the terrible doors; how sad the dunny
And the things you drew on the wall.

A VICTIM

Jan Tyssen, one of the four Dutch killed by Maori when Tasman anchored in Murderers' Bay in 1642

No prey for prowling keels, the south
We found a monster risky to rouse
That at the first approach bared teeth
And slew four with terrible blows.

I, Jan Tyssen, company's sailor,
Shipped aboard Zeehaen from Batavia,
Gerrit Janz master; signed to follow
Bully Tasman, lands to discover.

Java to Mauritius were orders, then
Southward far to the fabulous coast:
Glory to captains, to our masters gain;
To us reward as pleased them best.

Grim under earth the gale-black sea
Spat us between ice-tainted lips;
Heemskirck, Zeehaen, denied that way,
With fair winds eastward bore our hopes:

Mountains stood up (I, Tyssen, now
Remember all thickly through the black
Swoon of the savage's thrust) below
Clouted, thin lipped, a dull surf spoke.

This land we coasted, came on a bay
Calm where canoes slid slim at sunset;
Wary we waited, heard a hollow voice cry,
None came near, nor omen of onset:

Morning brought more canoes; we made
Offer of mirrors, good iron pots,
As orders were; but only the tide
Plucked by paddles, and hoarse shouts

Answered. I, one of seven, was told
'Take Zeehaen's boat, pull to your ship'.
(Ah, with what bells is my brain filled
That I forget!) We crossed the gap

Green between hulls. Like devils drove
Cruel of our kind the dark-limbed crew;
Blood bloomed and vanished where the wave
Mouthed for the fruit of us they slew.

I, Tyssen, first blood to the south,
Turned Tasman from that hateful haven.
Your history's cold, and cold's my death,
Past pity, past anger, past forgiving.

SESTINA

Not by voyages or accidents of ships,
Not by waves or the larger rhythms of the sea,
Are your islands mapped, measurable in Time;
Cook's fluent keel made crisp the bushy shore
Simple for seamen, but the projected life gropes
Where rocks in no chart rooted maliciously move.

Nebulae of ocean round which the thin tides move
Like a wavering of mist; here days are ships.
Under mountains, on beaches, a flat life gropes
After that taller dimension; beyond the sea,
Beyond the weeping reefs and sand-cragged shore,
Seeks some vertical structure, cities of the stature of Time.

Gulf'd from those tall cities, twice gulf'd from Time,
Strange even to each other these live and move
Where Waimakariri trowels the silted shore,
Where the harbours and foothills feed their seasonal ships;
Sure is the musterer's foot, safe the passage by sea,
But gust-crazed in gorges man unmeasured gropes.

On the wrong side of legend each man gropes
In the never-navigated currents of Time:
O even should the glittering surf fold back the sea
Far as the Americas, making fools of ships,
Still would the marooned in starving fancy move
Mountains all of glass on the Time-curved shore.

Wreckage mocks history, makes huts on the shore;
Continents pull like moons where the pilot gropes
By dials false to the day; island-bound ships
Wallow in treacherous gulfs this side of Time,
All instruments failing; stars indifferent move
Over fleets scattered on the dead-buoyant sea:

For since every sea has become a strange sea
Where cities and states founder, and every shore
Has dripping crevices where tide-creatures move,
From island to island man's dumb shape gropes
Hoping to recover some discarded gold by Time
Buried in beaches with the wooden bones of ships;

And now maps are folded, now infrequently ships
Counterfeit days, cruising off the fluid shore,
Can look-out leap, crying islands, solid in Time?

WILD IRON

Sea go dark, dark with wind,
Feet go heavy, heavy with sand,
Thoughts go wild, wild with the sound
Of iron on the old shed swinging, clanging:
Go dark, go heavy, go wild, go round,
    Dark with the wind,
    Heavy with the sand,
Wild with the iron that tears at the nail
And the foundering shriek of the gale.

SECOND SONG

Time who takes what he can use
   Takes our body and blood
For some enormous ignorant hour
Neither our fear nor fury chose;
Neither the purpose nor the power
Heaven might manage or accuse
   Lays ambush on this road.
     Now is the same as never
     Where Orion hangs head down.

Uttermost ocean like a mirror
   Images man's face
Screwed and dwarfed to island size,
Less wonder and more terror;
With peering prison-slitted eyes,
With madness marching nearer
   Than in a roomier place.
     Now is the same as never
     Where Orion hangs head down.

Shadows of cities, shadows of men
   Possess what Tasman found,
Shadows of shadows mock the old
Crime of nation tried again;
Shepherd and flock together sold
Straggle, and lean dogs whine
   On man's and no man's ground.
     Now is the same as never
     Where Orion hangs head down.

IT IS TOO LATE

It is too late
To be known, to be great;
Wire hoops the hills, and
Closed is the land:
Now it is absurd
To be seen, to be heard;
Nobody dreams of first,
Second, best, worst.

In no sense terrific
Or proud in Pacific,
Think a dropped cream-can
Will rouse Japan;
Discard the highest
Mountain, the dryest
Summer, the coppered steeple,
And the Maori people:
For these are only
Games for the lonely;
And the trader in freaks
Lost bottom seeks.

Walking weary
By the Waimakariri,
I cannot colour that stream
With wreck's red steam;
Nor picture shelter
Hell's crypt, fear-swelter,
But as stripe of pines
On brown skylines.

What the films show,
What the wires know
Is real, but who read
With nervous greed
Each stencil thrill,

Cry, Kill boys kill,
And of the most perilous
Post are jealous—
As if blood ran
Or breath were drawn
Or any seed sown
To be great, to be known.

DIALOGUE OF ISLAND AND TIME

Time: National, the word, is a sign among you,
Everywhere nation is talked and taught;
In one-man schools, at public luncheons,
They speak of a nation, never of islands,
As if by repeated incantation
Some god might be persuaded
To descend and transfigure,
Making every man bigger.

Island: The third and fourth generations
Begin to speak differently,
Suffering mutations,
Cannot help identity;
Nation's their only sign
Meaning man and brother,
Telling power, till Time
Discover another.

Time: Man and brother, power,
Flourishing in the same
Place in the same hour
Have no other name,
Till thought bravely stand
Where fear grimacing stood,
And the savage island
Renounce both power and blood.

Island: Show me, Time, behind
Your sea-dark curtain,
What is in your mind
Of which I may be certain,
Some luminous remote direction,
Fair wind and sky's protection.

Time: Step forward, Jew, from those
Of the nation God chose:

            Prophesy to the plains
            To the coast of heavy rains
            To the Waikato and the white
            New alps antarctic bright.

The Jew: Fierce nomadic enterprise
            Made me a nation;
            Came then God's enemies,
            Captivity, persecution;
            Babylon enslaved me,
            Islanded among
            Storms, doom'd to a sea
            Of infinite wrong.
            Bitter after exile
            I returned home,
            Yet in a little while
            Fell prey to Rome:
            Many were dispersed,
            Many renounced God
            Whose promise reversed,
            Like poison in the blood,
            Remained—

Island: You were promised too?
            We are exiled like you;
            But the Promise will come true.

Time: Pay attention to the Jew.

The Jew: Promise turns poison,
            Curses occur in prayers,
            When islanders seek a nation
            Thousands of years.
            Never be flattered by
            The white buildings, the roads:
            I had a temple high
            Whose inner room was God's;
            That pride to vindicate,

| | That glory to restore,
I am betrayed to hate,
Endlessly at war. |
|---|---|
| *Island:* | Surely there are others,
Brave men and brothers
Exalted by their nation
After a different fashion? |
| *The Jew:* | Long or short endurance—
There is no other difference.
Though gun and gas are stronger
My warfare is longer. |
| *Island:* | Ah, heroic, my friend,
Your independence to defend. |
| *The Jew:* | That is, war without end.
Long since I have sought peace
But my enemies, crazed
With fear, will not cease.
Pitifully I am amazed
Hearing islanders claim
A destiny and a name. |
| *Time:* | There speaks my oldest citizen.
Man and brother he knows,
Nation and power he knows.
My sea-curtain falls again.
What more need I disclose? |
| *Island:* | You think you have frightened me.
I demand the glory and the tragedy.
Call me New Zealand. The name
And the endless war I claim. |
| *Time:* | But your desired safe direction,
Fair weather and sky's protection?
The land was taken and is given, it will be the worse
To fabricate a promise that turns a curse. |

Island: Fold your sea-curtain. Look,
History has given me a book
Brighter than this ghostly conversation:
Land, power, and love of nation.

Time: The blasphemous interpreter
Pretending Time's ghostly sight
Deceives in the last chapter
Which I, not he, shall write;
Which I have already written
In no eventual sense:
Time writes, and has forgotten,
Before your books commence.

Island: Then, sir, if the books are lies,
What better can you advise?

Time: I have lifted my sea-curtain, have shown
In what wild waters God's chosen are thrown,
By what traces of torment a nation is known.

Island: Tasman found, Cook mapped;
Cities were planted, forests stripped;
Grandfather, father, and son
Have called me their own.
Surely there is something beyond
Plundering, possession of the land?
Show me some landmark feature,
Not the past again, but the future.

Time: You would get no further if I did.
The future from the past is hid.
What good would it do if I spoke
Words at which your ears would break,
Your eyes explode, your spirit die,
Confronting the eternal Why?

Island: I will not be frightened—

Time: Be safely enlightened
By ghosts, by actual presences.
Live and build, build and live,
Sing, repair your fences.
Nation is a hazardous sign
When great peoples expect
Mutation and, torn by Time,
That sign reject.
Let pity and love exclaim,
Meaning man and brother,
Telling power, till Time
Discover another.

NO SECOND COMING

Whose fancy fakes such crusted stuff
As sea's cold pickle keeps for ever
Betrays his blood to Time-in-death;
For him the island slims no lover
Nor shall Pacific's rhyming throes
Her belly-water break, from under
Five thousand miles of blossoming ooze
Venus be born with pearl and thunder.

SAILING OR DROWNING
1943

DISCOVERY

How shall I compare the discovery of islands?
History had many instinctive processes
Past reason's range, green innocence of nerves,
Now all destroyed by self-analysis.

Or, out of God the separated streams
Down honeyed valleys, Minoan, Egyptian,
And latterly Polynesia like ocean rains,
Flowing, became one flood, one swift corruption;

Or, the mad bar-beating bird of the mind
Still finding the unknown intolerable
Burst into a vaster cage, contained by seas,
Prisoned by planets within the measurable;

Or, Gulliver with needles, guns, and glass,
Thrusting trinkets up from the amazing hatches,
Luring doll kings and popes off palm-tree perches,
Sold them the Age of Reason from the beaches;

Dazzle no more in the discoverer's eye
When his blind chart unglazes, foam and flower
Suddenly spilt on the retreating mirror,
Landfall undreamed or anchorage unsure.

Compare, compare, now horrible untruth
Rings true in our obliterating season:
Our islands lost again, all earth one island,
And all our travel circumnavigation.

NINE SONNETS

I

IN MEMORIAM 2/LIEUTENANT T. C. F. RONALDS

Weeping for bones in Africa, I turn
Our youth over like a dead bird in my hand.
This unexpected personal concern
That what has character can simply end

Is my unsoldierlike acknowledgment
Cousin, to you, once gentle-tough, inert
Now, after the death-flurry of that front
Found finished too. And why should my report

Cry one more hero, winking through its tears?
I would say, you are cut off, and mourn for that;
Because history where it destroys admires,
But here if your blood's tongued it must recite

South Island feats, those tall snow-country tales
Among incredulous Tunisian hills.

II

OUT OF SLEEP

Awake but not yet up, too early morning
Brings you like bells in matrix of mist
Noises the mind may finger, but no meaning.
Two blocks away a single car has crossed

Your intersection with the hour; each noise
A cough in the cathedral of your waking—
The cleaners have no souls, no sins—each does
Some job, Christ dying or the day breaking.

This you suppose is what goes on all day.
No-one is allowed long to stop and listen,
But takes brief turns at it: now as you lie
Dead calm, a gust in the damp cedar hissing

Will have the mist right off in half a minute.
You will not grasp the meaning, you will be in it.

III

SAILING OR DROWNING

In terms of some green myth, sailing or drowning,
Each day makes clear a statement to the next;
But to make out our tomorrow from its motives
Is pure guessing, yesterday's were so mixed.

Papa, Atea, parents of gods or islands,
Quickly forgave the treacherous beaches, none
So bloodily furrowed that the secret tides
Could not make the evening and the morning one.

Ambition has annulled that constitution;
In the solid sea and the space over the sea
Explosions of a complex origin
Shock, rock, and split the memory.

Sailing or drowning, the living and the dead,
Less than the gist of what has just been said.

IV

POLYNESIA

Surf is a partial deafness islanders
All suffer from, committed to the land;
A resonant hades, traversing, the fathers
Left cold or sweltering a world behind;

A drumming, drumming, drumming till there leapt
Fully afforested from the well of ocean
Valley and peak; the glove of blindness clapped
On trusting eyes; perpetual collision

Indistinguishable in those eyes,
Of salt of tears within and spray without;
Currents not warm or cold, of abstract seas
By any sense unfathomed, but where float

Small gods in shawls of bark, blind, numb, and deaf,
But buoyant, eastward, in the blaze of surf.

V

THE NAVIGATORS

Oh rational successful hands that swept
Sea treasures up, by sunlight as in fog
Fumbling for islands, is there no wave big
Enough to wash your red ones green? Oh kept
In suavest history, gloved, quite dark how dipped
In red lagoons, the bright stain like a flag
Flowing and floating. Cradled in the vague
Currents where cables mumble murder slept

And sleeps, but dreams, hands that will not come clean
In endless dumb show utter what they did;
Because it was their rational violence
To think discreet discharge of guns would add
Island on island, that the seas would fence,
And time confirm them, in a change of scene.

VI

THE FALL OF ICARUS

The painting by Brueghel the Elder

The glistening coast, field-labour and sea-faring,
Stood like a crystal brimming with fine weather;
When he went down in flames all held together,
True to earth's ancient compact against caring:

The sun that flayed him warmed the ploughman's back,
The wind that stunned him swept the carrack on
Through the gay archipelago where none
Pitied or even noticed his bad luck.

Among the headlong pilots no revenge
Was wild enough for that indifference:
Wings flogged the fairway, made the seascape wince;
But when the flames that flagged each prouder plunge

Guttered, a mere breeze whisked off the stain.
At once the scenery was itself again.

VII

THE OLD PROVINCIAL COUNCIL
BUILDINGS, CHRISTCHURCH

The steps are saucered in the trodden parts,
But that doesn't take long to happen here;
Two or three generations' traffic starts
In stone like this to make time's meaning clear.

Azaleas burn your gaze away below,
Corbel and finial tell you where to stop;
For present purposes, it does to know
Transport is licensed somewhere at the top.

Children of those who suffered a sea change
May wonder how much history was quarried
And carted, hoisted, carved; and find it strange
How shallow here their unworn age lies buried

Before its time, before their time, whose eyes
Get back from a stopped clock their own surprise.

VIII

TO M. H. HOLCROFT

That silence in the hills suggested neither
Prayer Book nor Year Book nor our games could save us,
For all the manly noise we made together;
Plainly the mountain would not move or move us.

The dead were burying their dead so deep
No roots could reach them; mostly we behaved
As if the country shamed us with a shape
Too trite or terrible to be believed.

Now all the history that did not happen
Begins, and stings like an unfrozen wound;
Beaches are barbed, the obvious roads lie open
Towards those foothills, Monte, where you found

Spiritual powers, but root and rock to grip;
For islands, an intelligible hope.

IX

AT JOACHIM KAHN'S

A recording of a Beethoven quartet

Your 'innermost Beethoven' in the uttermost isles,
Half angel and half 'plane attains his peak
In weather like these southerlies that strike
But let your glass wall stand; his ceiling smiles;
He outclimbs all. Your room contains controls
To track in dazed skies an invisible wake
And pull his signals down just where you like,
It happens, among these unconnected hills.

The stone-deaf islands may resolve their pain
Easily, however distance howls them down,
By adaptation towards the albatross:
To rise on a stilled wing; or, on these tuned
Strings ride gales to patience; or, to cross
Motionless horizons as if not marooned.

SPRING, 1942

A letter to Sub-Lieutenant D. J. M. Glover, R.N.Z.N.V.R.

I walk to the Bryndwr bus
By the Wairarapa Stream,
Where a boy too young for an angler
Hooks trout too small to take;
With a Handel air in my head
(The radio just turned off)
And a book I shall not read
Because of the hills that hang
In the east, the shreds of thought and
Hopes that hang in my head.

I think, as I do now,
What do you think of islands
Who have made the formative journey
From antarctic to arctic—
Have laid yourself in the breech
Of this time's gun, to be fired
Into God knows what target?
In all that violent process
You follow the arc of islands.
The seas are shaping something.

In the bus rounding the river
Which the English think looks English
(Not reading between the willows)
I gaze through the jolting window,
Never expecting a symbol
To join our thought or reclaim
The undeniable oceans
That freeze or flame between us;
But you were the pine in the park,
The toughest, that we admired,
But could not establish the name.

And stopping between the colleges
Where over the mounded foliage
Of chestnuts, the six miles off
Hills shoulder the sun,
I wonder if half our worries
Were nineteenth-century Gothic.
These were the stones laid on us:
Did rebel imagination
Serve us no better than Samson's
Wrench, raving the roof down,
For building the City of God?

I did not expect a symbol,
Resigned to no sign given;
But the clock has stopped in the tower,
The ivy is stripped from the walls.
I have only to walk to work.
There is neither time nor money
For putting up sham pavilions;
Only the night's work
For me, battle or boredom
For you. Oh there will be poets
And there will be wars, and work,
And a child. You will return.

You wanted thoughts like the Arrow
River, and luminous
But never cold; you will have them.
'There is only hope for people
'Who live upon islands'—(no poet
Could mean just that, but something
Was in his mind at the time.)
All I can add in our case
Is, we do not choose our islands,
But mountains are magnets where
Our fathers sailed in under,
Heroes or hangdog exiles
Or (it doesn't matter) marooned.

The ivy is swept and burned
And the sallow clock has stopped
That would never keep good time.
One generation of exiles,
Two more of amphibious hauntings
Of beaches, and now this other
We needed to keep so badly.
Oh I could go down to harbours
And mourn with a hundred years
Of hunger what slips away there,
If that were not fearing the future.
Any day you may return.

RITE OF SPRING

Cold, limp with winter burial,
And mouldy with excessive rain,
My optimism shows no root
Now that I dig it up again.

Too easily the spade goes in,
Too heavily the spade heaves out;
A weekly tenant of the swamp,
I till in jest and plant in doubt.

I neither, between famous seas,
Dandle my idylls, island-graced,
Nor angrily enjoy a land
Not unequivocally waste.

Willow and lilac split the bud
And seagulls bray behind the plough:
This corm of courage shows no root,
The gilt is off that Golden Bough.

IN SUMMER SHEETED UNDER

In summer sheeted under
Acres of warm iron
We who drained our estate
Sleep in a wind, drying

The skin of our days,
Sucking our need of water
From private tanks, tapping
The secret strata.

Now is the confident season
For all exotic growth,
Fleshy of limb and leaf
Towards the blunted south.

Our clay is crusted, our
Tar sweats and shimmers;
Windows stand wide upon
The desert of summer's

Pride, pride of our time
In a little dry dust;
Men but not as trees, walking
Fast, wordless. In a mist.

PANTOUM OF WAR IN THE PACIFIC

*. . . if th' assassination
Could trammel up the consequence, and catch
With his surcease, success; that but this blow
Might be the be-all and the end-all here,
But here, upon this bank and shoal of time . . .*
                                                    MACBETH

The scale was blown up early in the piece.
To calculate what constitutes a thrill
Is harder than success from his surcease—
The casualities were few, the damage nil.

To calculate what constitutes a thrill
Hits home between the dreadful and the dread.
The casualties were few, the damage nil;
Numbers adjust the size of tears we shed.

Hits home between the dreadful and the dread
The atoll razed, the island changing hands.
Numbers adjust the size of tears we shed;
Nerves are the faculty that understands.

The atoll razed, the island changing hands,
With what explosions and what whisperings,
Nerves are the faculty that understands.
Daily death's rumour towers on sturdier wings.

With what explosions and what whisperings
Are vital points for any public statement;
Daily death's rumour towers on sturdier wings
Than life's canard content with fear's abatement.

Are vital points for any public statement
A frank design for death in true proportion?
Than life's canard content with fear's abatement
Nothing's more liable to plain distortion.

A frank design for death in true proportion
Is harder than success from his surcease—
Nothing's more liable to plain distortion.
The scale was blown up early in the piece.

LANDFALL IN UNKNOWN SEAS

*The 300th Anniversary of the Discovery of New Zealand
by Abel Tasman, 13 December, 1642*

i

Simply by sailing in a new direction
You could enlarge the world.
                          You picked your captain,
Keen on discoveries, tough enough to make them,
Whatever vessels could be spared from other
More urgent service for a year's adventure;
Took stock of the more probable conjectures
About the Unknown to be traversed, all
Guesses at golden coasts and tales of monsters
To be digested into plain instructions
For likely and unlikely situations.

All this resolved and done, you launched the whole
On a fine morning, the best time of year,
Skies widening and the oceanic furies
Subdued by summer illumination; time
To go and to be gazed at going
On a fine morning, in the Name of God
Into the nameless waters of the world.

O you had estimated all the chances
Of business in those waters, the world's waters
Yet unexploited.
                  But more than the sea-empire's
Cannon, the dogs of bronze and iron barking
From Timor to the Straits, backed up the challenge.
Between you and the South an older enmity
Lodged in the searching mind, that would not tolerate
So huge a hegemony of ignorance.
There, where your Indies had already sprinkled

Their tribes like ocean rains, you aimed your voyage;
Like them invoked your God, gave seas to history
And islands to new hazardous tomorrows.

ii

Suddenly exhilaration
Went off like a gun, the whole
Horizon, the long chase done,
Hove to. There was the seascape
Crammed with coast, surprising
As new lands will, the sailor
Moving on the face of the waters,
Watching the earth take shape
Round the unearthly summits, brighter
Than its emerging colour.

Yet this, no far fool's errand,
Was less than the heart desired,
In its old Indian dream
The glittering gulfs ascending
Past palaces and mountains
Making one architecture.
Here the uplifted structure,
Peak and pillar of cloud—
O splendour of desolation—reared
Tall from the pit of the swell,
With a shadow, a finger of wind, forbade
Hopes of a lucky landing.

Always to islanders danger
Is what comes over the sea;
Over the yellow sands and the clear
Shallows, the dull filament
Flickers, the blood of strangers:
Death discovered the Sailor

O in a flash, in a flat calm,
A clash of boats in the bay
And the day marred with murder.
The dead required no further
Warning to keep their distance;
The rest, noting the failure,
Pushed on with a reconnaissance
To the north; and sailed away.

iii

Well, home is the Sailor, and that is a chapter
In a schoolbook, a relevant yesterday
We thought we knew all about, being much apter
    To profit, sure of our ground,
No murderers mooring in our Golden Bay.

But now there are no more islands to be found
And the eye scans risky horizons of its own
In unsettled weather, and murmurs of the drowned
    Haunt their familiar beaches—
Who navigates us towards what unknown

But not improbable provinces? Who reaches
A future down for us from the high shelf
Of spiritual daring? Not those speeches
    Pinning on the Past like a decoration
For merit that congratulates itself,

O not the self-important celebration
Or most painstaking history, can release
The current of a discoverer's elation
    And silence the voices saying,
'Here is the world's end where wonders cease.'

Only by a more faithful memory, laying
On him the half-light of a diffident glory,
The Sailor lives, and stands beside us, paying
    Out into our time's wave
The stain of blood that writes an island story.

ATTITUDES FOR A NEW ZEALAND POET

I

That part of you the world offended so
Has atrophied, or else your strategy
Has changed, or else you have so much to do,
The simplest way is seeming to agree.

The falling cities, bones, the brutal sky
And waste land botany do not recur.
Now, it is not an easy question why
You were ashamed that things were as they were.

Come world, poor Tom-world, and let us reason
Together, settle down and take our time:
We shall have bomber and bud in the same season,
Music and malice both in the one rhyme,

Thunder and tears; committed at this stage
Neither to horror nor a horrible age.

II

World, up to now we've heard your hungers wail
No more than mock alerts; a South Seas moon
Unspeckled by our deaths can safely sail,
Escorted by our Never past our Soon.

The great sad duchess by a trick saw pass
Shapes of her husband and her children dead;
But farther off, darker than in a glass,
The natural body of our grief is read.

Men of our islands and our blood returning
Broken or whole, can still be reticent;
They do not wear that face we are discerning
As in a mirror momentarily lent,

A glitter that might be pride, an ashy glow
That could be pity, if the shapes would show.

III

*The Skeleton of the Great Moa
in the Canterbury Museum, Christchurch*

The skeleton of the moa on iron crutches
Broods over no great waste; a private swamp
Was where this tree grew feathers once, that hatches
Its dusty clutch, and guards them from the damp.

Interesting failure to adapt on islands,
Taller but not more fallen than I, who come
Bone to his bone, peculiarly New Zealand's.
The eyes of children flicker round this tomb

Under the skylights, wonder at the huge egg
Found in a thousand pieces, pieced together
But with less patience than the bones that dug
In time deep shelter against ocean weather:

Not I, some child, born in a marvellous year,
Will learn the trick of standing upright here.

JACK WITHOUT MAGIC
1946

JACK WITHOUT MAGIC

Cleverer than ever you busy brain,
Nature you dread, and next to nature, art:
Jack without magic springs his traps in vain
Against these giants and genii of the heart.

DIMENSIONAL

The oil the blue
Peculiar gleam
Is on, not through
The beer-brown stream;

Flat viscous flow,
Vein of the valley;
The sun should know
How hotly shallow

That mirror skin
That sliding shape
Whose sandflies sing
The never deep;

Whose gusty flies
In a windless air
Repeat the song
In the earth's ear:

Hot and thin, and
Hot and shallow

Shakes the sand
And looks the yellow

Glimmering stone
Under the stream;

We have seen
How these become

Thin and hot,
A different shape

The oil the blue
The never deep.

Picton, 1938

CHILDREN, SWIMMERS

Children, swimmers, the whole brilliant harbour
Coveting the young bodies, how far drowned
Under the wrack-curdled tide of my mind
You are, and you fellow-swimmer deeper

Than all since I, envying every bead of the sea
Jewelling your skin, its passionate regard shining,
Coveted barely with a look, complaining
With a gooseflesh my numb thought in the warm day:

And saw the days pass, and upon the shrunken
Soot-sprinkled pool-green harbour the days pass:
O but how under sea glitters no less
Your flesh against time's fathoms, and not sunken

Ever, astonishes with a breath this drowned
Valley where tides are lost and love's dead found.

PARADISE REVISITED

Milton made Eve his blonde, but she is dark
And dark is Eden where her tree ascends;
And yet she shines; no shy deer in God's park,
She's formidable. The fruit between her hands

Is moon to her deliberate earth; the cold
Smooth yellow rind of moon or fruit invites
Tongue, or on branch alight allures handhold.
Temptress, to darken her delights

Offers her apple with one withering leaf,
Ripeness and death in hand; imparts that knowledge,
Yet firm and lovingly lets in the thief
Of innocence: moon-sodden foliage

Parted, lays her big limbs unshadowed bare
To the white clamberer's prehensile stare.

SELF-PORTRAIT

The wistful camera caught this four-year-old
But could not stare him into wistfulness;
He holds the toy that he is given to hold:
A passionate failure or a staled success

Look back into their likeness while I look
With pity not self-pity at the plain
Mechanical image that I first mistook
For my own image; there, timid or vain,

Semblance of my own eyes my eyes discern
Casting on mine as I cast back on these
Regard not self-regard: till the toy turn
Into a lover clasped, into wide seas,

The salt or visionary wave, and the days heap
Sorrow upon sorrow for all he could not keep.

THE WAKING BIRD REFUTES

Rain's unassuaging fountains multiply
In air on earth and leaf. The Flood began
This way, listened to at windows by
The sleepless: one wept, one revolved a plan,

One died and rose again, one felt
That colder breath blow from the poles of lips
At love's meridian. This way now the spoilt
Firmament of the blood dissolves and drops;

The bright waste repossessive element
Beats barely audible, one sound imposing
Silence upon silence. This way I went
To pull our histories down, down, heavens accusing

Of rainbowed guile, whose penal rains descend.
But the waking bird refutes: world will not end.

UNHURT, THERE IS NO HELP

When was it first they called each other mine?
Not in Donne's day: by then their love had grown
Or shrunk from Phoenix into spider, sign
Of sinner turned addict. Love, be your own

And stay the far side of that Tree
Whose seed struck earth between us; give again
A bite of apple; do not mind if He
Is somewhere in the garden, or that pain

Is frost or blight and the leaf blackens.
That is your birthright and redeeming sin.
Unhurt, there is no help for her who wakens
Puzzled, her sole power gone, in the obscene

Daffodil bed where the decrepit knees
Promised speech from heaven, and could barely please.

DUNEDIN

for James K. Baxter

Is it window or mirror the enormous
Deforming glass propped on horizons here?
What did we see? Some town pinched in a pass
Across which stares perpetual startled sheer
Vacuous day, the kind blind wilderness,
Space put behind bars, face pushed too near:

Painfully upright among lost hills
Bowed under cloud, made fast to the shocked ships
Locked in an eddy, dwelling. There, none wills
Redress or dreams it, or pondering some lapse
Out of a dream strays back into that town
A mirage of the cracked antarctic stole,
Or stumbles on the original dazed stone
Pitched out of Scotland to the opposite Pole.

TO D. G. OVERSEAS

Little at present, but to promise you
This morning, the still island, waking wholly
Like Adam from the bride-sleep, all things new;
Not a shout yet, or plane, these few
Bees out on summer Sunday morning early
Play bombers over parks and domes of bloom;
The Port Hills fallen in canvas folds that soon
The winking windscreen spangles. Home
Huddled like this would wake and day begin
Hardly noticing that you had come in.

1942

DARKNESS, PATIENCE

Darkness, patience at the root of the tree;
One bloom exhausted drops, or a lopped hand.
O premature my legend, flowered and fallen,
Winter has whipped that colour from the land.
Darkness, patience in the blood that hides
Its unborn springs, runs colder but not sullen.

AT DEAD LOW WATER
1949

AT DEAD LOW WATER

i

At dead low water, smell of harbour bottom,
Sump of opulent tides; in foul chinks twirl
Weed and whorl of silt recoiling, clouding
The wan harbour sighing on all its beaches.

The boat was not deliberately abandoned
But tied here and forgotten, left afloat
Freakishly, bobbing where the summers foundered,
Jarring each wave the jetty's tettered limbs;

Worm carves wave polishes original shapes,
Bolt and knot give way, gaps in the decking
Turn up again, driftwood on other sands.
All drifts till fire or burial.

Life, trapped, remembers in the rancid shallows
What crept before the enormous strides of love
When the word alone was, and the waters:
Goes back to the beginning, the whole terror

Of time and patience. Keel and bolt are frilled
With the shrimp's forest, all green-bearded timbers.
Salt rocky chink, nude silted cleft give off
Birth smell, death smell. Mute ages tread the womb.

ii

Nervous quiet not calm possesses
Sea water here, the wave turns wary
Finding itself so far inland.

The father with the child came down
First thing one morning, before any
Dreamt of visiting the beach; it was

Daylight but grey, midsummer; they
Crossed high-water mark, dry-shod,
Derelict shells, weed crisped or rotting,

Down to the spongy rim, slowly
Without fear, stepping hand in hand
Within an inch of the harmless sea

Pure, unfractured, many miles,
Still steel water sheathed between
Once violent hills, volcanic shapes.

O memory, child, what entered at the
Eye, ecstasy, air or water?
What at the mouth? But carefully

Morning by morning incorruption
Puts on corruption; nervously
Wave creeps in and lingers over

Tideswept heaps where the fly breeds:
Memory flows where all is tainted,
Death with life and life with death.

Twenty years. A child returned
Discerns in quicksand his own footprint
Brimming and fading, vanishing.

iii

Failed at the one flood we do not count
On miracles again, and you may say
We die from now; while each amazed migrant
Waves back, and cannot tear his eyes away

From his own image, the weeping threatening
Accusing thing, and knows death does not rid
Him even of the deformed sunk sifted thing,
Memory's residue; because the dead,

Father and child, still walk the water's edge:
A kindness, an inconsequent pastime, froze
In time's tormented rock, became an age
When tropics shifted, buried rivers rose,

Meaningless but for individual pain
No death, no birth relieves or lunar pulses drown.

Governor's Bay, December 1944

TOMB OF AN ANCESTOR

I

IN MEMORIAM, R.L.M.G.

The oldest of us burst into tears and cried
Let me go home, but she stayed, watching
At her staircase window ship after ship ride
Like birds her grieving sunsets; there sat stitching

Grandchildren's things. She died by the same sea.
High over it she led us in the steepening heat
To the yellow grave; her clay
Chose that way home: dismissed, our feet

Were seen to have stopped and turned again down hill;
The street fell like an ink-blue river
In the heat to the bay, the basking ships, this Isle
Of her oblivion, our broad day. Heaped over

So lightly, she stretched like time behind us, or
Graven in cloud, our farthest ancestor.

II

TO FANNY ROSE MAY

Great-aunt, surviving of that generation
Whose blood sweetens the embittered seas between
Fabulous old England and these innovations
My mountainous islands: in the bright sad scene

I praise with you your voyage, and hers who sleeps
A sister folded in the hill cemetery,
Sacrifice or seed lodged on those slopes
That seem barbaric, by the unworshipped sea

Toward which she would shade her eyes. I know the fires
That forged the harbour and the heights glow still,
A million years old memory, but there's
Neither memory nor world here but that hill

Where struck your voyaging sister seed, from whom
I grow, and this praise flows, this blood, this name.

FOUR DESCRIPTIONS AND A PICTURE

I

GENESIS

Original sea, no breath or bird, your eyes
Nourished their unborn sun; upon the face
Of waters wary of love I moved: I praise
The evening and the morning. Now your voice

Made birds of the dumb salt, I heard
Aeonial Phoenix and interpreted,
'Be fire in me, be death and birth'; the third
Day pain was made, we saw that it was good,

Walking with difficulty, speech failing,
On the hill passing the stone pillar, man
And woman sole on earth, erect or falling,
Compelling, pitying. Trumpets the next dawn

Sounded above the levelled flood: we came
To the Garden, giving each beast and tree a name.

II
WITH HOW MAD STEPS

Nightwatchman in some crater of the moon—
No, not that lunatic
But the dumb satellite itself, my tune
The cold sphere's silence; and I stick

(Abiding, law-abiding) to that orbit
Fire once described, tossed into space to cool
From my earth's body; a gyrating habit.
What if she watches? She'll

Mask with the mirror of her tides those shores
Her flesh makes in the heavens, and even
While dawn destroys me her young foliage stirs;
Neither is mathematical space forgiven

My dear earth's distance, though her heart descry
With how mad steps, her moon, I climb the sky.

III

SHE SITS WITH HER TWO CHILDREN

She sits with her two children in the holy evening,
You find your way there over the bare mountains,
Her mirror's landscape mild, the beasts deceiving
With heart's trick sword and cloak. Her rigid fountains

Timeless their shining seed to time let fall
Where the root screams for death. She has spread a table
For the foretold prince who will
Strike blind her mirror with a kiss, the bubble—

Her high blood's iridescent sphere—send down
In a mist, her mortal dew, naked deliver
Her from her cage of waters. There alone
With her two children the goldhaired and the clever

She waits for the armed angel, bird or breath
Descending, out of the mirror leaning, death.

IV

THEN IF THIS DIES

Then if this dies, by so much we die too,
Blood has been shed before
And when the heart was dry the brain would go;
But this one beats, and stings his nerve the more

Because death finds him in a waiting torment
Lancing a straw hope against that steel
Night's disappointment
(Their starved lips in the room;) the fall

Of leaf, or house that glacier groaning
At frightful pressures, never was her step
(Listening till morning):
For so we die, and do not stop

Loving or dying, so we wait
Indoors; death has not finished with us yet.

V

ALL DARKENS BUT HER IMAGE

The door stood wide, she stood
Between those pillars of the sea:
She leaned against the evening light,
Mountains no taller than her knee,
The first star at her breast, her eyes
Turned where the top of heaven should be.

All darkens but her image there.
What was the god's disguise?—the far
Pacific dims, she is alone
Where no more sea shall be, or mar
Her gaze with tears, nor blood defile
The virgin mother of a star.

OLD HAND OF THE SEA

Old hand of the sea feeling
Blind in sunlight for the salt-veined beaches
O setting on a tide my bearded boat a-sailing
Easy as the bird's breast that barely touches

Immemorial deeps of death:
Here, now, my harbour, child's play pool,
Sifter of sunk bright treasure, breaker of earth,
Is monster and lover of the gazing soul.

Horizons bloomed here on the globes of eyes,
Here grieving fog fastened those lids with tears
Disfiguring, transfiguring; holidays
Nested like bird or girl. All disappears

But the salt searching hand. Oh sightless tides
What blossom blows to you from spring hillsides?

EDEN GATE

The paper boat sank to the bottom of the garden
The train steamed in at the white wicked gate,
The old wind wished in the hedge, the sodden
Sack loved the yellow shoot;

And scampering children woke the world
Singing Happy Doomsday over all the green willows
That sprang like panic from the crotch of the cold
Sappy earth, and away in the withered hollows

A hand no warmer than a cloud rummaged
At the river's roots: up there in the sky
God's one blue eye looked down on the damaged
Boy tied by the string of a toy

And saw him off at the gate and the train
All over again.

MUSIC FOR WORDS

To Douglas Lilburn

No ancient singing dancing infancy
Made luminous, made wise our island earth;
No tongue is suddenly sweet, no foot steps free,
The sneer at natural joy will pass for mirth.

If on the street a rhythmic speech is heard
Ears prick, heads turn towards the foreign clown
Whose musical greeting's like a waking bird:
They fear great Pan will bankrupt half the town.

A whip for these dead heels to make them dance!
Once I had nothing better to suggest,
As if blood could be got out of the dry bones:

But since you sang my words I count on most
Music, and a heroic eloquence
To remake man out of this chattering dust.

LILI KRAUS PLAYING AT CHRISTCHURCH

A poem for Lili Kraus—
But the word could not imitate the winged
Instrument, or so build with hands the house
Not made with hands, although it longed

For breath and bone like this, the sound
Made flesh to dance and die; a music blown
To unburn Troy on the sea-deafened ground.
You do not dance alone

Or hold no hand, here on the beautiful
Coast where seas and mountains dazzling turn
Their face of thirst: the dull
Heart flames, the Wanderer's forlorn

And listless 'Where?' is answered, as he hears
Love like a bird sing in her tower of tears.

July, 1946

A SONATA OF SCHUBERT

You move to the piano. What is it we know?
You have taught your hands to die;
All that we have to and most fear to do
Now to be done, sufficingly,

If hands could call the lapsed soul again
With music's trumpet-silences to witness
The mortal marvel of its joy and pain.
It is the falling brightness

From keen unusual skies, omen of birds,
Day breaking at the beach of sacrifice.
We are strange, strange to ourselves. Who is it applauds
His own transfiguring? Who plays?

Not you, not we—this, we had never dreamt,
These hands between us and the heavens' contempt.

March, 1947

POEMS
1949-1957

A LEAF

The puzzle presented by any kind of a leaf,
One among millions to smudge your airy sceneries
Or among millions one your window tickler
Gust upon gust agitates, a trifle sharp
Enough to murder sleep:

Shape of a leaf, shine of a leaf,
Shade of a leaf yellow among yellow leaves of
The prophet Micah with a slip of perished silk
Marks nothing, still is a character, a syllable
Made flesh before the word:

Bud of a leaf, blade of a leaf
Given a strange twist, given for something to do
With deadly baffled fingers happy to squeeze
Blood from a conundrum: insoluble but endlessly
Amusing in the attempt.

TO FORGET SELF AND ALL

To forget self and all, forget foremost
This whimpering second unlicked self my country,
To go like nobody's fool an ungulled ghost
By adorned midnight and the pitch of noon
Commanding at large everywhere his entry,
Unimaginable waterchinks, granular dark of a stone?
Why that'd be freedom heyday, hey
For freedom that'd be the day
And as good a dream as any to be damned for.

Then to patch it up with self and all and all
This tousled sunny-mouthed sandy-legged coast,
These painted and these rusted streets,
This heart so supple and small,
Blinding mountain, deafening river
And smooth anxious sheets,
And go like a sober lover like nobody's ghost?
Why that'd be freedom heyday, hey
Freedom! That'd be the day
And as good a dream as any to be damned to.

To sink both self and all why sink the whole
Phenomenal enterprise, colours shapes and sizes
Low like Lucifer's bolt from the cockshied roost
Of groundless paradise: peeled gold gull
Whom the cracked verb of his thoughts
Blew down blew up mid-air, where the sea's gorge rises,
The burning brain's nine feathering fathom doused
And prints with bubbles one grand row of noughts?
Why that'd be freedom heyday, hey
For freedom, that'd be the day
And as good a dream as any to be damned by.

IDYLLS IN COLOUR FILM

I

CRISTOBAL

Top to bottom of a skin white wall
Some thin vine blossom bleeds, the sun
Indolently erodes the sill.
Blood can run cold in this hot town.

And the blue sky bends a very smooth look
And the water keeps malignant calm
And the itchy mouth the Canal has makes
Lips to compress their ocean's arm.

Fat with colour the day commands
Holstered, blazing boss of the street.
Time daren't stir, nor the four winds.
Death is detained, but won't be late.

Cool off at El Tropico; fans,
Cans, fans and a glassful which
Can't go bad like the barrow man's
Bag of oranges while you watch.

Polyglot, polychrome droop or blow
Lush hybrids of the dollar shallows.
Nylon blooms and rags in a row,
Negress purples, negress yellows

Shame without shock of step or breast
Pale casual trash two hours ashore;
From bodily darkness have digressed
By a flowery shift of skins, no more.

Now continents and oceans lie
Farther than planets, and the scarlet
Or bruise-blue petals kiss your knee,
Romancing in an isthmian twilight

Of temperate islands.
                     The Zone Troops
Strike MacArthurian attitudes.
Avid the traveller slums the shops,
Tickling a vein which no blood leads

That street where one was knifed last night.
Home and aboard is where to be,
With a mast-high moon, eyes crackling bright.
The Caribbean's the next sea.

II

CURACAO

The slimed embrasures of old fortress walls
Green lower-lipped outside Saint Anna Bay
Cannot articulate: this hoarse wind smells
Of oil; two hundred tankers night and day

Hod El Dorado past the Bridge of Boats
Up the foul stream and down. The Dutch facades
Cold and small as coral are the sights
Most photographed: but memory knows no aids

One mile from Willemstad (past midnight, that
Refiner's fire across the basin mimes
Hell but fools nobody) while we set foot
Again on the low desolate slope whose name's

Nothing and nowhere: fingering the leaf-shuttered
Inconsequence of streets. For the wind here's
Close and vigilant, misses no flitted
Grain or leaf, watches each step, cares

For every stone in Hoogstraat.
                              Have we lived
Anywhere if not here, walking alone
Through dreams or deaths awake, having arrived
One hour ago, by morning to be gone?

ELEGY ON MY FATHER

Tremayne Curnow, of Canterbury, New Zealand, 1880-1949

Spring in his death abounds among the lily islands,
There to bathe him for the grave antipodean snows
Fall floodlong, rivermouths all in bloom, and those
Fragile church timbers quiver
By the bourne of his burial where robed he goes
No journey at all. One sheet's enough to cover
My end of the world and his, and the same silence.

While in Paddington autumn is air-borne, earth-given,
Day's nimbus nearer staring, colder smoulders;
Breath of a death not my own bewilders
Dead calm with breathless choirs
O bird-creation singing where the world moulders!
God's poor, the crutched and stunted spires
Thumb heavenward humorously under the unriven

Marble November has nailed across their sky:
Up there, dank ceiling is the dazzling floor
All souls inhabit, the lilied seas, no shore
My tear-smudged map mislimned.
When did a wind of the extreme South before
Mix autumn, spring and death? False maps are dimmed,
Lovingly they mock each other, image and eye.

The ends of the earth are folded in his grave
In sound of the Pacific and the hills he tramped singing,
God knows romantically or by what love bringing
Wine from a clay creek-bed,
Good bread; or by what glance the inane skies ringing
Lucidly round; or by what shuffle or tread
Warning the dirt of miracles. Still that nave

He knelt in puts off its poor planks, looms loftier
Lonelier than Losinga's that spells in stone
The Undivided Name. *Oh quickening bone*
Of the Mass-priest under grass
Green in my absent spring, sweet relic atone
To our earth's Lord for the pride of all our voyages,
That the salt winds which scattered us blow softer.

London, November 1949

WHEN THE HULK OF THE WORLD

When the hulk of the world whirls again between
Us for the ships shift me where your dusk is dawn
    My skyblue side of the globe,
Where the mooncast squid's eye of a downcast ocean
Goggles till it gets me in the beam of its brine—
    Oh then, sweet claustrophobe
I leave among the lost leaves of a London wood
(So dark, we missed the middle of our road)
    Can spring condone, redeem
One treachery of departure from that life,
Shiftless to fetch this love?
    Seas will be seas, the same;
Thick as our blood may flood, our opposite isles
Chase each other round till the quiet poles
    Crack, and the six days top
Totter, but catch us neither sight nor hold;
Place will be place, limbs may not fold
    Their natural death in dreams.
I pray, pray for me on some spring-wet pavement
Where halts the heartprint of our salt bereavement,
    Pray over many times,
Forgive him the seas forgive him the spring leaf,
All bloom ungathered perishable as grief,
    For the hulk of the world's between
And I go as a ghost, one flesh I and the wind
That lifts us both so lightly, but so bound
    Never to be ghost alone.

THE EYE IS MORE OR LESS SATISFIED
WITH SEEING

Wholehearted he can't move
    From where he is, nor love

Wholehearted that place,
    Indigene janus-face,

Half mocking half,
    Neither caring to laugh.

Does true or false sun rise?
    Do both half eyes tell lies?

Cradle or grave, which view's
    The actual of the two?

Half eyes foretell, forget
    Sunrise, sunset,

Or closed a fraction's while
    Half eyes half smile

Upon light the spider lid
    Snares, holds hid

And holds him whole (between
    The split scarves of that scene)

Brimming astride a pulse
    Of moon-described eyeball's

Immobile plenitude—
    Flower of the slight stemmed flood.

Snap open! He's all eyes, wary,
    Darting both ways one query,

Whether the moonbeam glanced
    Upon half to whole enhanced,

Or wholly the soul's error
    And confederate mirror.

IN MEMORY OF DYLAN THOMAS

*And the Lord God formed man of the dust of
the ground, and breathed into his nostrils the
breath of life; and man became a living soul.*

Never a talking but a telling breath
Fanned fire from clay upright to the tip of his tongue,
Who burning to tell told all the days of his death
It was the ghost alive in a beast's lung
Panting for-ever out.
Now the five gates are shut,
The grassy fingers sheathed in enough dust,
And the last work, at most, is what all must.

He hardly knew what struck him the first spark
Bursting the bolts of sense upon the frame
Of things. It was light outraging the pure dark.
It was the ghost buried alive in time,
Purse-lipped for pain,
That blew upon his brain
The iridescent sweaty swarms that rose
Winged imagos, out of their wormy throes.

Adam and Eve beneath the village bethel
Played snakes and ladders. Bibles were hot to touch;
He laid his open on the cool of a sill, the wrath all
Feared he fondled; fruit-in-hand, found such
Were all men's bedfellows.
And he could never close
Genesis for appleblossom's joy, our tripping
First girl and boy in plucking time caught napping.

Self-scrutineer, with what pierced eyes he pored,
Live coals upon the body's private inches.
Shame in the ghost rebuffed what flesh adored,
But the game beast on a griddle heaved its haunches:

Sinful, infinitely worth
Saving, the beasts of earth
At the end of their tether either way, that fled
Between the matin-bell and midnight bed.

> *And he said, What hast thou done? the voice of thy
> brother's blood crieth unto me from the ground.*

A town boy, he trod
The earth beneath the pavements
And knew stones could bleed.
Storming bereavements
Inflamed his eyes. He was afraid

With the common fear that time
Of a blitzing sickness,
But under blood and blame
Exclaimed, so blazed his darkness,
Genesis' thunderbolt shot home.

Irrational good, caged
In faith's condemned cell, burning
Its own breast unassuaged—
Crybaby crying the morning
Stars out while Creation raged.

> *And out of the ground the Lord God formed
> every beast of the field, and every fowl of the
> air; and brought them unto Adam to see what
> he would call them; and whatsoever Adam
> called every living creature, that was the
> name thereof.*

Laugharne village peters out an inch from the fishy bay
Whose rackless tides lightly incuriously rap their twice-a-day
Reminders to hewn human stone deaf as cockle shells
That a lifeless landscape suckles, fills and flushes the salt wells,
And the moon is a spirit.

                        By day by dead pearl calm
He valued the mere view of it the bare sea-moulded arm
Relaxed about slack water. Southward the ship shape
Of the shade of an isle is Lundy. Some lounging cape
Condescends to the vanishing west; a few miles that way brings
You, map-witted, to Pendine Sands.
                              Mere living things
Crackle their moments out over the breath-heavy green
Foreshorelands, glimmers of godhead not unseen
But often to crawl, creep, scamper, flit or fly,
Starting under his feet in the track of his eye
Who named them, with praise again as Adam unfallen had,
Praise that never to Adam fallen the Maker forbade.
Named the heron son of Zebedee fishing his moody shoal.
Named the congregation of crabs, dabs, waterbirds, the owl
So fell to fur, the ranger fox outsnapping a winter's cold.
Named, who never could have told
The tally of his heart's household.

> *A window shalt thou make to the ark, and in a cubit shalt thou finish it above: and the door of the ark shalt thou set in the side thereof; with lower, second, and third storeys shalt thou make it.*

A stack of whitewashed stone
Cramped square upon a lap of rock
And butted endwise to a bushy bluff,
One chink of the foreshore there,

The house—locally known
As Boathouse—house enough
Or Ark at flood-time fit to bear
Pigeon-postman Noah and all his stock.

> *And the Lord smelled a sweet savour: and the Lord said in his heart, I will not again curse the ground any more for man's sake; for the*

imagination of man's heart is evil from his youth: neither will I again smite any more every thing living, as I have done.

Sir John's Hill. Bramble and scrubby growth
Humped not much higher than chimney-puff.
By tide-scurf, dead weed, up and over the path
Ramble, far-fetching scholar, the brief rough

Prose of a broken landscape, summoning how
On this earth, out of all rare wringers
Of hands and hearts one here saw heaven's bent brow
Pitifully judging birds and singers.

'Ware the hawk, 'ware the hill,
Claw clenched for the trilling throat,
The shadow, the shudder, the kill,
Feathers afloat—

But in the map of mercy among a city's
Dying millions he fell,
Who chose of heaven's thousand thousand pities
The sparrow's one, and all.

KEEP IN A COOL PLACE

A bee in a bloom on the long hand of a floral
Clock can't possibly tell the right time
And if it could whatever would the poor bee do with it
In insufferably hot weather like this?

Everything white looks washed, at the correct distance
And may be the correct distance. You could eat
Our biggest ship sweet as sugar and space can make her.
Every body's just unwrapped, one scrap of a shaving

Left for luck or the look, the maker's seal intact,
Glad to be genuine! The glassy seaside's
Exact to the last detail, tick of a tide,
Fluke of the wind, slant of a sail. The swimmers

On lawns and the athletes in cosy white beds have visitors
And more flowers. Poor bee! He can make up time
At frantic no speed, whether tick or tock,
Hour or minute hand's immaterial. That's

Exactly how it is now. It is. It is
Summer all over the striped humming-top of the morning
And what lovely balloons, prayer-filled (going up!) to fluke
For once and for all the right time, the correct distance.

TO INTRODUCE THE LANDSCAPE

To introduce the landscape to the language
Here on the spot, say that it can't be done
By kindness or mirrors or by talking slang
With a coast accent. Sputter your pieces one

By one like wet matches you scrape and drop:
No self-staled poet can hold a candle to
The light he stares by. Life is the wrong shop
For pictures, you say, having all points and no view.

Ponderous pine wagging his wind-sopped brushes
Daubs Latin skies upon Chinese lagoons.
What tides leak through the mangroves and the rushes
Or lofted, wash long needles and large cones?

And where, from here, do you go? Out with the tide
You won't, without some word that will have lied.

JACK-IN-THE-BOAT

is always ready to row across the bath or lake.
Wind up the motor, and watch him dip his
blades like a true oarsman—in, out, in, out—
with never-tiring enthusiasm.
              LEGEND ON A TOY-MAKER'S PACKAGE

Children, children, come and look
Through the crack in the corner of the middle of the world
At the clockwork man in a cardboard house.
He's crying, children, crying.
He's not true, really.

Once he was new like you, you see
Through the crack in the corner of the middle of the night,
The bright blue man on the wind-up sea,
Oh, he went so beautifully.
He's not true, really.

O cruel was the pleasure-land they never should have painted
On the front and the back, the funny brand of weather,
For the crack in the corner of the middle of the picture
Let the colours leak away.
He's not true, really.

One at a time, children, come and look
Through the crack in the corner of the middle of the day
At Jack-in-the-Boat where the light leaves float.
He's dying of a broken spring.
He's not true, really.

MEMENTOS OF AN OCCASION

Wallace Stevens, 1879-1955

i

Dead but to the world, Stevens, do you find
The anecdotes lucid there, compared with these?

And what comparisons with your style when crossing
Composedly the blue thresholds to sit down
Oceans away (because all airs bore alike
And Indian-wise an alien offshore fragrance)—
Or mulch with moist real hands the seedy words
To bear in season as fresh-cut coxcomb blooms
As anyone else's green and god-sown country
Whose natives, planting and watering botany books,
Had their disappointments?

                   Can they be less alien
Or more at home, the breath-stopped kiss-shaped nomenclatures
Down where the dead are?
                       If we have all met somewhere
Elsewhere before?

ii

      A well-set-up shade passed
Forth between ranting sun and rabble retina,
Announcing a prim masque, a conducted illusion
Out of worse nothing.

              It was not quite as if
The snake, uniquely accomplished, could slip in and
Out of the time-worn pelt experience till
Crackle! and lastly dry scurf popping
Nipped up thin air, dumbfounded all as-ifs—

iii

Let that have been as it may, you are the type
Should manage a vaporous shift of habitat
To where, if any can raise a squeak yours may be
Intelligible, as ghostliest counsel goes,
As poems, the ponderable these, are eligible,

iv

Capable to detect where reality was not
And scrupulous what to put in place of it.

SPECTACULAR BLOSSOM

Mock up again, summer, the sooty altars
Between the sweltering tides and the tin gardens,
All the colours of the stained bow windows.
Quick, she'll be dead on time, the single
Actress shuffling red petals to this music,
Percussive light! So many suns she harbours
And keeps them jigging, her puppet suns,
All over the dead hot calm impure
Blood noon tide of the breathless bay.

Are the victims always so beautiful?

Pearls pluck at her, she has tossed her girls
Breast-flowers for keepsakes now she is going
For ever and astray. I see her feet
Slip into the perfect fit the shallows make her
Purposefully, sure as she is the sea
Levels its lucent ruins underfoot
That were sharp dead white shells, that will be sands.
The shallows kiss like knives.

Always for this
They are chosen for their beauty.

Wristiest slaughterman December smooths
The temple bones and parts the grey-blown brows
With humid fingers. It is an ageless wind
That loves with knives, it knows our need, it flows
Justly, simply as water greets the blood,
And woody tumours burst in scarlet spray.
An old man's blood spills bright as a girl's
On beaches where the knees of light crash down.
These dying ejaculate their bloom.

Can anyone choose
And call it beauty?—The victims
Are always beautiful.

EVIDENCES OF RECENT FLOOD

Adam and Eve and Pinch Me
Went down to the river to bathe,
Adam and Eve were drowned,
And who do you think was saved?

I

LOGBOOK FOUND ON ARARAT

Only one night the
     squall made a great show,
thunderclaps fit to burst,
      mightily flapped
linens and lightnings,
     heaven's menagerie leapt
loose upon decks
    and the herd snarled below.

Calm yawned by dawn
      assuaged our seafaring
staring by some land's lamp
      outlimbed, so gloomy,
less than it loomed a
     withering gulf could show me,
but snuffed-out beacons
     uncaring, uncuring:

blindalleyed seaways,
     suburban promontories.
Dogging a dumb spark,
     diamond in the spine
(dead by my reckoning
     both the red and the green),
my only ship shaped home
     lonelier than seas

pattering at the prow
                        between pouring deeps:
fearfully at flood-peak
                        unfathomed my ark
the dove-watch kept
                        in cages of wickerwork,
bickering and bloody
                        the beaks and claw-tips:

no not fair-feathered
                        upon the first isles
these cage-birds thwarted
                        at each other's throats;
though landward upon a lipping
                        liquor she floats
and flood no more now
                        than upon sands prevails.

Groping for moorings
                        the grave side of dawn
God! horrorstruck we see
                        from what hoodwinking hidden
wrecks gasped the rescued
                        grew some certainty
love soiled some shore yet
                        Oh some sheer crown

of the earth rage overlooked
                        I look-out stared
at mirrorstricken my own
                        land manfully back:
all I steered mists to gain by
                        drowning, luck
or the All-Duplicity on
                        high had spared:

    the cocks crescent
                    upon crags and sills
    the seed surgent in
                    brine-sodden furrows
    the girl congealed in smiling
                    salt, all sorrows
    shambling, All-Shallows
                    in a slough of souls.

None here could drown
                    though thou God jerk the bells
unfathomable steeplejacked
                    rungs below:
mockers when thy rains wreathed,
                    ripe mockers now,
the obsolete polyp
                    sobbing in their skulls:

and their lame talk pursues
                    prediluvian lines
and all weather or never
                    is thy Name's news spoken
and those mortal talons
                    of the dove not mistaken
and thy deluge a dribble
                    whose drunken ebb sucks
a bald earth born to us
                    of shipwreck, hooks
by the gills on Ararat,
                    grounded for our pains.

II

THE CHANGELING

Once where the leaky
                  islands and the lame
swimmers ducked
                  and draked between earshots
of stars and oceans
                  there plummeted a fulgent
freak with unwebbed
                  fingers, a girl kind of
fish whose fire and
                  water works and bellied
moon waxing in the summer
                  seascape bared
(with her light like ashes
                  of a god absconded)
our home hill-toppled town
                  grown cold as wishes.

Lithe she unlocked
                  the circuit of the harbour
tickled she fore and aft
                  the daft old sulking
bottoms, with her tail tipped
                  many a green
mooring-chain, diving in a
                  weedy boy's skull
her small bell sang.
                  Such miracles of the lovers
and fishes followed her
                  that sodden straw
sparked, sat up and glared like some
                  god-bonfired navy
most classically scuttled, glory's
                  dredges dismasted.

Swim! spied our laddery
      town from all its rungs;
corks, bladders and the last
      breath beat the surges;
till her sunken silver
     filleted in the main
of mankind wilted
     on the bright tide's verge.
Hooked and played
     and laid upon the sands
loose she lay
     under the yellow lupin.
Cold fell the quiet coast,
      midnight looming
and the midnight ebb
     and when it struck she rose

up lightly, her stains
     were silken, she shook out
her hair in the teeth of the
     tide's thunder so
idly that the moon
     sank without a cry
nor dared we more than dumbly
      trail her tiny
mortal steps deep down
     to the town train.
Listen! those whistles
     down our line to the grave.
Listen! those bells
     that toll the changeling home
ding at the ebb, ocean,
     dong at the flood.

Sob, shabby islands
     in your dull weeds doting
On a fleeting fable
     a feather in the sun.
All your white horse
     wishes would not wash
one white shell from the
     wave the changeling swam.
She's home and dry
     and high among the ladders
as plain as daylight that's
     back like an old debt,
drowned swimmers in her eyes
     and stars, and oceans,
her comb and her glass
     and her ticket in her hand.

HE CRACKED A WORD

He cracked a word to get at the inside
Of the inside, then the whole paper bag full
The man said were ripe and good.
The shrunken kernels
Like black tongues in dead mouths derided
The sillinesses of song and wagging wisdom.
These made a small dumb pile, the hopping shells
Froze to the floor, and those made patterns
Half-witted cameras glared at, finding as usual
Huge meteorites in mouseland.
What barefaced robbery!
He sat, sat, sat mechanically adding
To the small dumb pile, to the patterns on the floor,
Conscious of nothing but memories, wishes
And a faint but unmistakable pricking of the thumbs,
The beginnings of his joy.

A SMALL ROOM WITH LARGE WINDOWS
1962

A SMALL ROOM WITH LARGE WINDOWS

i

What it would look like if really there were only
One point of the compass not known illusory,
All other quarters proving nothing but quaint
Obsolete expressions of true north (would it be?),
And seeds, birds, children, loves and thoughts bore down
The unwinding abiding beam from birth
To death! What a plan!
                  Or parabola.
You describe yours, I mine, simple as that,
With a pop and a puff of nonchalant stars up top,
Then down, dutiful dead stick, down
(True north all the way nevertheless).

One way to save space and a world of trouble.

A word on arrival, a word on departure.
A passage of proud verse, rightly construed.
An unerring pen to edit the ensuing silences
(That's more like it).

ii

        Seven ageing pine trees hide
Their heads in air but, planted on bare knees,
Supplicate wind and tide. See if you can
See it (if this is it), half earth, half heaven,
Half land, half water, what you call a view
Strung out between the windows and the tree trunks;
Below sills a world moist with new making where
The mangrove race number their cheated floods.
Now in a field azure rapidly folding
Swells a cloud sable, a bad bitching squall

Thrashes the old pines, has them twitching
Root and branch, rumouring a Gotterdammerung.
Foreknowledge infects them to the heart.
                              Comfortable
To creak in tune, comfortable to damn
Slime-suckled mangrove for its muddy truckling
With time and tide, knotted to the vein it leeches.

iii

In the interim, how the children should be educated,
Pending a decision, a question much debated
In our island realms. It being, as it is,
Out of the question merely to recognize
The whole three hundred and sixty degrees,
Which prudence if not propriety forbids,
It is necessary to avail oneself of aids
Like the Bible, or no Bible, free swimming tuition,
Art, sex, no sex and so on. Not to direct
So much as to normalize personality, protect
From all hazards of climate, parentage, diet,
Whatever it is exists. While, on the quiet,
It is understood there is a judgment preparing
Which finds the compass totally without bearing
And the present course correct beyond a doubt,
There being two points precisely, one in, one out.

iv

A kingfisher's naked arc alight
Upon a dead stick in the mud
A scarlet geranium wild on a wet bank
A man stepping it out in the near distance
With a dog and a bag
                    on a spit of shell
On a wire in a mist
                    a gannet impacting
Explode a dozen diverse dullnesses
Like a burst of accurate fire.

AN OPPRESSIVE CLIMATE, A POPULOUS NEIGHBOURHOOD

i

I look from this back window straight across
To that back window and there see standing
In the through-current rippling his white vest and briefs
A grey-headed man who turns, retreats, returns
(For the coolness, no doubt, of linoleum to the naked sole)

And looks from that back window straight across
To this back window and there sees standing
In the through-current naked but for my white briefs
A brown-headed man. Put it that we note and respect
Each other's individuality, he is not chagrined

Because I am content with briefs and reject the vest,
Nor is my own free spirit offended because he
Cannot comfortably acquiesce. This inspection complete,
I too turn from the rear and pad the apartment through
(For the coolness, truly, of linoleum to the naked sole)

To the street-front window and there see a brown-thighed girl
Crotched on a ground-floor sill. One up and to the right
A blue nightgown bodilessly gets out of bed
And passes from view. A boy rearranges his pillow.
I pan to the flight above, a hand shifts a pot-plant

From the sill, one hand, the perfection of anonymity.
What we cherish is our own business, this hand innocently
Withdraws its treasure. Put it simply that the owner may be stripped
Naked for the heat and has nothing to hide but himself.
Satisfied, I put no impertinent question to myself

Concerning these companions, least of all any literary question.
Hell, let's face it, is horribly hot and overcrowded,
But where else do you find the niceties of neighbourly regard

More observed and the mitigable nuisance of neighbourly love
Better understood than in this City we have been building so long?

ii

A dog howls all morning Saturday.
His inhuman frequencies
Touch like sad art with its astonishing
Human unlikenesses.

Somebody tied the poor dog up
In the hinder-precinct of some brownstone,
And shut the door and the garden gate
And went out, and left him alone.

Thickly in this thick heat the dog
Ululates, convoking the neighbours, say,
500 to 600 East 84th and 85th streets,
To tell of some too far away

Catastrophe, some canine Cathay
Scourged by earthquake or famine—
Some disaster in Canis Major our myopic
Instruments cannot examine.

Dog, dog, I'm tied up too.
Be my guest, my metaphor.
Be Fool to my Lear till the neighbours hear
And maybe open the door.

The dog howls. It's a dog howling.
If it warbled, it would be a bird.
If we don't make ourselves intelligible,
We make ourselves heard.

Dog, dog, they will come and untie you.
You shall have a pat and a bone,
And a run with the Gracie Square dogs
To whom you are personally known.

My telephone doesn't ring of itself—
That calls for the human hand.
Dog, dog, all it takes is patience,
Which dogs don't understand.

East 85th Street, New York, July 1961

TREES, EFFIGIES, MOVING OBJECTS
1972

TREES, EFFIGIES, MOVING OBJECTS

I

LONE KAURI ROAD

The first time I looked seaward, westward,
it was looking back yellowly,
a dulling incandescence of the eye of day.
It was looking back over its raised hand.
Everything was backing away.

Read for a bit. It squinted between the lines.
Pages were backing away.
Print was busy with what print does,
trees with what trees do that time of day,
sun with what sun does, the sea
with one voice only, its own,
spoke no other language than that one.

There wasn't any track from which to hang
the black transparency that was travelling
south-away to the cold pole. It was cloud
browed over the yellow cornea which I called
an eyeball for want of another notion,
cloud above an ocean. It leaked.

Baldachin, black umbrella, bucket with a hole,
drizzled horizon, sleazy drape,
it hardly mattered which, or as much
what cometing bitchcraft, rocketed shitbags,
charred cherubim pocked and pitted the iceface
of space in time, the black traveller.
Everything was backing away.

The next time I looked seaward,
it was looking sooted red, a bloodshot cornea
browed with a shade that could be simulated
if the paint were thick enough, and audible,
to blow the coned noses of the young kauri,
the kettle spout sweating,
the hound snoring at my feet,
the taste of tobacco, the tacky fingers
on the pen, the paper from whose plane
the last time I looked seaward
would it be a mile, as the dust flies,
down the dulling valley, westward?
everything was backing away.

II

FRIENDSHIP HEIGHTS

By night by fishes' light
I am absently walking in another summer,
a stranger here myself. The streetlamps
and the headlamps hang and swim in waves
greened round, quite extraordinarily like
a fish-tank forest. Presently I shall see
deep avenues there, extraordinarily like
a neighbourhood called Friendship, another time.

On the sidewalk an iron receptacle
NOT FOR THE DEPOSIT OF MAIL.
This other one is the right one
FOR U.S. MAIL, the hollow lovers' tree
black as a thought of the world inside.

Receptacle, receive me, receive me.

Each cave is calm as if no traffic stormed,
the six-lane fugue is lost on the deaf leaf.
Cave, storm, fugue, forest could be very like
a neighbourhood called Friendship: only semblances
are lost on the black hollow iron tree
and the deaf leaf gurgles to itself by night
by fishes' light. Another semblance might
be absently walking, in another summer,
extraordinarily like the goodness, say, of God,
something scented *and weeping in the evening dew.*

The zoo closes,
the horned owl dozes,
his dinner is done
and the bunnies are dead,

the green runs red,
see how they run
underneath the water where the sharks do fly
my, oh my!
underneath the water where the sharks do fly.

III

AN UPPER ROOM

Where is the world? Upstairs.
At the end of the corridor. The last room.
I have drawn the curtains back, under the window
I am waiting for my students, my sixty-first
year is high cloud that alters as it filters
the sun, good light while it lasts, for reading.
I can hear them growing up the stairs.

Goosey goosey gander
Whither do you wander?

Our book is open. Volcanic islets visit
over the top of the tide which is full, and full
of dead men's images, pouring into the room
Through the dear might of Him that walk'd the waves.
(Could you do that? Keep clear of the margins.
Here my line starts and it finishes *here*,
no later than the light lasts.)

We speak only
to each other but as if a third were present,
the thing we say.

Smaller than thought can think
the hours between us shrink,
books wink, volcanic islets sink
below that brink,
black margin, blind white ink.

There I found an old man
Who wouldn't say his prayers.

Dead bunnies. Blinded teddy bears.

IV

AGENDA

A man who has never visited the Uffizi isn't educated. English remark.

Be a playboy at 35. South British Insurance. Picture of man fishing, from boat, with bottle.

Enjoy sex and stop breeding. Message to the age from the Doctors Kronhausen, on waking.

V
DO IT YOURSELF

Make it what height you like, the
sky will not fall nor will the dead
president rise because of his
```
               O
               B
               E
               L
               I
               S
               K
               5
               5
               5
               f
               t
                .
```
nor is it any wonder that it is
one measured mile down river to the
```
               P    I
             A        T
           C    O        L
```
one measured mile up river to the
```
             L I N C
             M     O
             E     L
             M     N
             O R I A L I
             N C O L N M E
             M O R I A L I N
```
With a few simple tools the handyman
can erect his thought upon Waiheke, volcanic islet,
lat. 37S long. 175E for the time being.

Read the instructions carefully.

VI

NAMES ARE NEWS

A wood god botherer stands
not fifty feet from his own
door, calls trees by name.

Speak up we can't hear you.

Metrosideros robusta,
the northern rata. Usually
commencing life as an epiphyte
becomes a tall, massive tree
60 to 100 feet high.

Louder please.

Flowers are broad, dense,
terminal, many-flowered cymes,
dark scarlet.

What?

Dark scarlet.
Don't lean that weight! I call.
Shall I make you feel the full
rigour of a description?

Close!

For godsake no.

Closer.

Lord, I am small.
I break easily. I call
red cumulus green bubbled
cloud with a bloody curd,
not flowers, not cymes.
How fast do I have to talk?

Talk.

Seed vessels fly
forty thousand feet high
jetting towards a dark
destination up, up!
Funny how the sexual jets
grumbling aloft resemble
cymes, dark scarlet.
Can a machine do more?
Tall, massive clouds,
thunderheaded trees,
don't commence life that way.
Green pod, sky boring jet
nevertheless resemble.

Birds whistle and shit.

Lord,
I cannot compel you,
I implore you, by the dust
of a rigorous description
cracked by its own rigour,
lean easier, for the sake
of a chance resemblance.

Dark stays. Light goes.

Dark scarlet, inhuman,
silent in the fly-simmering
January sunlight
suffers no disguise,
description, resemblance.
A wood god botherer darkens
a moment his own doorstep,

enters, writes quickly,
adds a postscript.

The *New Zealand Herald* comes
late here, with the milk.
That was last week, the
pathologist's evidence
described the dead brother's
body, the burned-out farmstead,
what fat was burned away,
what skin, what battering the
skull *sustained* before the
Fire. And the oil-feed.
And the living brother by the rigour
of a description *stood
erect,* and the Court covered its
embarrassment, and ours, by the
rigour that was its only
rigour, of a description.

Flowers are broad, dense,
terminal

Louder please.

Jetting towards a dark
destination up, up!
It's a long long fall and a crack like doom
between the martinis and the satchels
up there and the dark down here.
Far too many flies, birds, worms, to begin with,
and that's not the end.

No.

VII

A FAMILY MATTER

Adam was no fool. He knew that at his age
a man must plan for his retirement. Or else.
He saw no better way than back to the bush.

An image in disrepair could study itself
in a pool, or such distraction from itself
as a bird flashing a scale upon his ear.

There was Cain to take over the business. There were signs.
Light no fires. Discharge no firearms.
Ten acre block for sale. Your private kingdom.

Lianes noosed harmlessly, the water ran
down above and below the road ran down
primevally babbling. Close to the foot

of a young totara, *Podocarpus hallii,*
Adam stumbled, and very nearly fell
over an old survey peg, half rotted.

If it blew like the wrath of God it was all blown over
ages ago, the angel hooked it, having lashed
round with a sword in a flaming bad temper.

Regeneration, conservation, were words
with which he comforted his mind, if angels,
vandals, vermin, got muddled in his mind.

Cain used to come over at the week-ends
and bring the children, who loved it.
Something must be done with it when the old man went.

VIII

THE KITCHEN CUPBOARD

Sun, moon, and tides.
With the compliments of the *New Zealand Herald*
and Donaghy's Industries Limited makers
of the finest cordage since 1876.
Look on the inside of the cupboard door,
the middle one, on the left of the sink-bench.

All the bays are empty, a quick-drying wind
from the south-west browns the grey silt
the ebb-tide printed sexily, opulently,
making Nature's *art nouveau*, little as it matters
to mudlarking crabs and the morning's blue heron.

Olive, olive-budded, mangroves wait for the turn,
little as it means, to call that waiting.

A green car follows a blue car passing a brown car
on the Shore Road beyond the mangroves which wait
no more than the tide does because nothing waits.
Everything happens at once. It is enough.

That is not to say there is nothing to cry about,
only that the poetry of tears is a dead cuckoo.

The middle one, on the left of the sink-bench.
I stuck it on with cellotape. Not quite straight.

IX

A DEAD LAMB

Never turn your back on the sea.
The mumble of the fall of time is continuous.

A billion billion broken waves deliver
a coloured glass globe at your feet, intact.

You say it is a Japanese fisherman's float.
It is a Japanese fisherman's float.

A king tide, a five o'clock low, is perfect
for picking mussels, picking at your ankle-bones.

The wind snaps at the yellow-scummed sea-froth,
so that an evanescence of irised bubbles occurs.

Simply, silverly the waves walk towards you.
A ship has changed position on the horizon.

The dog lifts a leg against a grass-clump
on a dune, for the count of three, wetting the sand.

There is standing room and much to be thankful for
in the present. Look, a dead lamb on the beach.

X

A FRAMED PHOTOGRAPH

The renaissance was six months old.
All the Kennedys were living at that time.
Jackie was hanging pictures in the White House.
I figured he could use the experience, Jack hornered,
when he starts in legal practice, naming Bobby
for Attorney-General.

Act one, scene one,
of the bloody melodrama. Everyone listened
while everyone read his poems. *BANG! BANG!*
and we cried all the way to My Lai.

To be silverly framed,
stood on the Bechstein, dusted daily
by the Jamaican girl whose eyes refuse them,
seeing alien Friendship one prolonged avenue
infinitely dusted, is a destiny which simply,
silverly they walk towards, towards my chair,
what jaunty pair
smiling the air
that flutters their trousers on Capitol Hill?
Why, Hiroshima Harry and the dandy Dean,
dust free. Heavenly muse!
fresh up your drink and sing.

What, exactly,
did he do at the Pentagon? He guessed he was
a deputy assistant secretary of defence,
a political appointment, modestly confided.
Hospitably home at cocktail time he took
one careful gin and tonic, excused himself
to mind State papers.

Dust the Bechstein, Anna.
Dust the megagothic national cathedral.
Dust destiny.

Fresh up. There is plenty of ice.

Receptacle, receive me.

XI

TWO PEDESTRIANS WITH
ONE THOUGHT

Things are things carried
away by the wind like this
big empty carton which
bumps as it skids as it
arse-over-kites over
anything else that's loose
dust, for instance, while
> *all the little angels*
> *ascend up ascend up*

things are things emptied
on the tip of the wind
arsey-versey vortically
big print for instance
APPLE JUICE nothing in the
world ever catches its
carton again where the
wind went ƎƆIUɾ ƎlddA
loose as the dust or the
water or the road or the
blood in your heels while
> *all the little angels*
> *ascend up on high*
> *all the little*

God!
That was close, that bus
bloody nearly bowled the
both of them the dog with his
hindleg hiked and
APPLE JUICE bumped off the
wind's big boot
> *angels*
> *ascend up*

hang on there

as long as you can
you and your dog before the
wind skins the water off the
road and the road off the
face of the earth
           on high
       which end up?
        Arse end up
full beam by daylight
this funeral goes grinning, a
lively clip, a tail wind, the
grave waiting
hang on to your hands
anything can happen
once where the wind went
fingers you feel to be
nailed so securely
can come loose too
hold on to your ears and
run dog run while
simply, silverly
they walk in the wind that is
rippling their trousers
Hiroshima Harry and the
dandy Dean
dust free dusted while
    all the little angels
    ascend ascend up
with
Plato in the middle
holding out his diddle in the
way souls piddle from a
very great height and
dead against the wind,
dead against the wind.

XII

MAGNIFICAT

Who hasn't sighted Mary
    as he hung hot-paced
by the skin of the humped highway
    south from Waikanae
three hundred feet above the
    only life-size ocean?
Tell me, mother of mysteries,
    how far is time?

Twelve electric bulbs
    halo Mary's head,
a glory made visible
    six feet in diameter,
two hundred and forty-five feet
    of solid hill beneath.
Tell me, mother of the empty grave,
    how high is heaven?

Mary's blessed face
    is six-and-a-half feet long,
her nose eighteen inches,
    her hands the same.
Conceived on such a scale,
    tell me, Dolorosa,
how sharp should a thorn be?
    how quick is death?

Mary's frame is timbered
    of two-by-four,
lapped with scrim and plastered
    three inches thick.
Westward of Kapiti
    the sun is overturned.
Tell me, Star of the Sea,
    what is darkness made of?

Mary has a manhole
    in the back of her head.
How else could a man get down there
    for maintenance, etc?
Mary is forty-seven feet,
    and that's not tall.
Tell me, by the Bread in your belly,
    how big is God?

I AM THE IMMACULATE
    CONCEPTION says
Mary's proud pedestal.
    Her lips concur.
Masterful giantess,
    don't misconceive me,
tell me, mother of the Way,
    where is the world?

XIII

A FOUR LETTER WORD

i

A wood god bothering cantor
rolls out his call. He names

tanekaha, kaiwaka, taraire.
Mispronounced, any of these

can strike dead and dumb. Well spoken,
they are a noise neither of the writhing root

nor glabrous leaf nor staring flower,
all that can unspeakably supervene.

ii

Tane mahuta is a very big tree,
because of the signboards at the roadside.

Tired trunk, punky at the heart,
disyllabic Tane is too venerable

for words. True, that at a given sign
they stop their cars and walk no distance

to have seen, to have found themselves,
as advertised, in the absence of the god,

to have decently exposed some inches of film
in honour of his great girth.

Strike him with lightning!
the old arboreal bore.

Cut him up for signboards. Just look at that,
such longevity, such bulk, such value in board feet.

iii

Titans were titanic in the old days
before the defoliant Thunderer.

The children had no fathers then, as now.
No nativity ode for Tane. At his namegiving

nobody had the time, having time only
short of an unspeakable supervention

to blurt him, Logos begotten of log,
the disyllable, as he came.

iv

In the technologies nothing can be done
without a divine sub-contract:

this one for the felling, the hollowing,
prone canoe, erected post;

Tane demiurgos,
lord of an obsolete skill:

not to keep an old man ticking
with a dead boy's heart

(cut while warm, after the crash,
pray for this tissue not to be rejected);

an instance now, look at it like that,
of what can unspeakably supervene,

ever since like cats in the dead of night
the first heaven and the first earth

coupled and begot,
and the theogonies littered the place

with the lordliest imaginable
stumps. That's life. That's fear

of this unspeakable that smashed the mouth
open, stamped on the balls and

ripped from the tongue's root, womb syllabled,
Tane, Tane mahuta.

XIV

BOURDON

Spring thunder thumps on Friendship,
    high hands divide, collide,
let lightning down and wet the town,
    blinding the riverside
where Lincoln stares but never sees
what Washington is up to.
That cloud-cuffed shaft, those stony knees,
heaven's thunderstruck antipodes
    discover, arse-end up too.

The matrix cracks, the god still born
    stares his measured mile,
marble trousered, marble browed,
    throned in classical style.
Stone eyelids grind, a stony throat
    chokes with cherry bloom.
The matrix cracks again, again!
Sifting riverwards in the rain
a slow detritus dusts the brain
    under a sunless dome.

Thunder is a bluejay cock and a hen
    and a roll of the wrists,
the gods alone are solid stone
    dressed like beasts.
Rain courses down the stone, the stairs,
    and the knees that wear
stone still, a stony gaze is
snug as a bullet, smooth as phrases,
    the well plugged sepulchre.

XV

A HOT TIME

They were doing their thing in the burning fiery furnace,
you couldn't hear the flute, harp, sackbut, psaltery
and all kinds of music for the silence of the flames.
Everything was very quiet in the heart of the furnace.

The wine was red, the acrylic was vermilion,
the pictures on the walls were hanging by their nails.
The needle was a diamond paddling in the bloodstream
issuing from the heart of the silence of the furnace,

streaming where it paddled in the stream that it was,
homing on the centre never to be punctured.
All the holy children were dancing on the needle
doing nothing but their thing in the burning fiery furnace,

Shadrach and Shakeback and Meshach and Sheshach
and Abednego and gay to bed we go along and upwards
of a hundred holy children in the burning fiery furnace.
It was dead still and silent at the centre of the disc.

There was the golden image, balls to the golden image,
balls to Nebuchadnezzar the king who set it up.
Not a note was audible over the silence of the flames,
of the psaltery and the dulcimer and all kinds of music.

Came the holy cold of morning, with all kinds of music
raking out the furnace, when their thing was done,
and which child broke silence, squeaking from the ashes,
issuing from the music of the flute, harp, etc.,

Shadrach or Shakeback or Meshach or Sheshach,
or gay to bed we go along with Abednego or who?
growing up the stone stair, issuing from the music,
sucking on a diamond like an apricot stone, saying

There I found an old man who wouldn't say his prayers,
I took him by the sackbut and threw him down the stairs,
I adore Doctor Logos, but Yeats is so mysterious,
because he doesn't communicate *like* Shakespeare *does to me.*

XVI

THERE IS A PLEASURE IN THE PATHLESS WOODS

When the green grenade explodes, does the kauri
experience an orgasm of the spent cone?
What is the king fern doing with its hairy knuckles?
Wildling and epiphyte, do they have problems too?
There's a reason for the spastic elbow of this taraire.
Look hard at nature. It is in the nature
of things to look, and look back, harder.
Botany is panic of another description.

XVII

LONE KAURI ROAD

Too many splashes, too many gashes,
too big and too many holes in the west wall:
one by one the rectangles blazed and blacked where the
sun fell out of its frame, the time of the day
hung round at a loose end, lopsided.

It was getting desperate, even a fool could see,
it was feverish work, impossible to plug them all.
Even a fool, seeing the first mountain fall
out not into the sea or the smoking west but into
the places where these had been, could see the spider
brushed up, dusted, shovelled into the stove, and
how fast his legs moved, without the least surprise.

A tui clucked, shat, whistled thrice.
My gaze was directed where the branch had been.
An engine fell mute into the shadow of the valley
where the shadow had been.

XVIII

ANY TIME NOW

Extraordinary things happen every day
in our street only this morning
the ground opened at my feet
without warning
unless it was a cloud in the south
balled like a swelling in the mouth.

And the air was fresh, being winter
time when the ground broke
disclosing a billion bodies burning
under a thin smoke.
Was it then that I saw in my walk
an eggshell, a capsicum stalk?

Such details are always so terribly
(if that is the word) distinct
as grit under the eyelid, like today
when the ground blinked,
disclosing what never should be seen.
Walking is a pleasure, I mean.

Fortunately there was not very much
traffic and no kiddies playing,
couldn't have picked a better day for it
I was just saying
when the ground closed over the sky
hollow as the cloud was high.

AN ABOMINABLE TEMPER
1973

TO THE READER

Look for my finger prints.
Good luck to you. I wore
no gloves when I burgled
your house and made off with
as much as I could carry,
a precious little. Now
I give myself up, what's in it
for you? All yours,

little as you knew or stared
or dreamt, the night I stole
in my stockinged face and feet,
shitscared you'd wake and catch me,
when I whipped your skinny wallet,
your ten-dollar watch, pearls
of more pearliness than price.
You missed them, did you?

All losses are loss,
life itself the most trifling
some experts testify.
Hardly less precious, then,
to get your own back now,
a little, a little the worse
for wear, a restitution.
It's that, or nothing.

A WINDOW FRAME

This paper is eleven and three-quarter
inches long, eight and one-quarter inches
wide, this table four feet five inches long,
thirty-two inches wide, this room

twelve feet square, this house one
thousand square feet, this window encloses
two leafless peach branches on which I count
fifty twigs and then give up, one mile

away the morning sunlight whitens or darkens
what I take to be the walls of houses
and the roofs along a long ridge of the land.
I should be used to it by now, the refusal

to move an inch closer, an inch to the right
or left or (so long as I look) to dismantle
the hallucination of fact, the refusal even
to speak, to explain, as if it were unpardonable

mortal sin on my part not to have remembered.
Am I to burn in my chair for no worse fault
than pulling out the plug? Am I to bear
an eternal blame because the Pacific Ocean

disappeared down the pipe and sucked the sky
down with it? The edges of this sheet
of paper are beginning to brown, slightly,
but there is no definable smell of burning

in this house, this room. This window encloses
two leafless peach branches on which I count
fifty twigs and then give up. It will be the
fifty-first on which a sparrow settles,

cock sparrow, he picks under each wing
distinctly, so many times for the left,
so many for the right, one loses count.
He is not there now nor will be yet.

I should be used to it, the way numbers
won't go by numbers, the injustice of it
that finds me guilty. A sparrow has not fallen
to the ground. Do you smell burning?

ii

It is not what you say,
it is not the way you say it,
it is not words in a certain order.

Look out the window.
                      It is on the page.
Examine the page.
                      It is out the window.
Knuckle the cool pane.
                      It is in the bone.
Why is the mud glassed,
                    with mangroves
bedded in the glass?
                  Why is the cloud
inverted in the glass?
                Why are islands
in the Gulf stained blue
              grained green with
interior lighting
        by Hoyte?
                Why not?

TO AN UNFORTUNATE YOUNG LADY WHO AFTER ATTENDING SIX PUBLIC READINGS BY THIRTY POETS ASKED, DOES ANYONE CARE?

How right you are, my dear.
Let us make an example of poetry.
It is possible, even for poets,
to live without it, so many do,
and to live with it, most of the time
impossible.
        Isn't it the mumble
of something loose behind,
or a fumble
in the back seat of the mind?
Or an innumerable company
of the heavenly host crying
rhubarb rhubarb rhubarb rhubarb
with *obbligato* innumerable other
syllables in several languages,
some dead?
        Does anyone care?
One man's rhubarb is another man's
artichoke and that's the reason why
the poetry of earth is never dead
dead dead.
        Rhubarb to you,
my dear, with cornflakes and cream,
every glorious carefree day and night of your life.

THIS BEACH CAN BE DANGEROUS

The fatalities of his nature cannot be disentangled from the fatality of all that which has been and will be. NIETZSCHE

WARNING
They came back, a well known face
familiarly transfigured, lifelikeness only
cancer, coronary, burning, mutilation
could have bestowed, they came by millions
and a friend or two calling me by my name
and my father, by a name no other could know.

BATHE BETWEEN THE FLAGS
Each with the same expression, his own,
mirrored in the sand or the mind, came back
the way they went calling like winter waves
pick-a-back on the humped horizon they rode
the strong disturbed westerly airstream
which covered the North Island.

DO NOT BATHE ALONE
It was their company that made it possible
for me to walk there, cracking the odd shell
with the butt of a manuka stick,
happy to the point of hopelessness.

TO DOUGLAS LILBURN AT FIFTY

My fiftieth year had come and gone. So Yeats,
in the course of one astonishing poem,
letting the fact drop, his timing perfect.

Toothless warriors, nonagenarian burgesses,
mumble the sweet cake, the spittled crumbs.
Somebody will blow out all the candles.

If you had your way, would you compose a score
with fifty bass drums gunning the day down
in self-salute? What do we expect?

A poor look-out for honest pastrycooks,
all the same, for the economy generally.
Come on, be a quinquagenarian!

It is only for one day. No two are alike.
Each has its singular fascination.
You are fifty only once.

The lightest of touches on the shoulder, this
unreckonable reminder, will it alter
the weather even a shade?

The written score affirms
shades, alterations, novelties,
the days and the midnights between the days:

in part, you will be persuaded to allow,
the music affirms, makes room at least
for silence to loom in

larger than in the hills where it first harboured,
eavesdropped upon, spied upon.
The idea was never to break it!

Is it fiddlers' armpit sweat, the punished
bellies of drums, bespittled brass,
cock-pitted against silence?

Is it bloodbeat, waterdrop, all manner alchemical
electronic tinctures? *'Tis magic,*
Magic that hath ravish'd me!

Hang up blonde promontories, MacDiarmid's oils.
Take down my book, some poet's attitude.
Set a silence to catch a silence.

Eavesdropper, what are you overhearing now?
Blow out the candles. Praise the cake.
Indulge the birthday guest.

1965

WHAT WAS THAT?

Now I heard in my dream
  or dreamt I heard
    the Last Trump
      it was not loud
seraphic brass
  made nobody jump
    sing glory glory
      or the damned scream

it was not loud
  more of a hum
    than a vocal murmur
      a unison
without voices
  no star performer
    blowing up the graveyards
      tooting on a cloud

it was the single sound of
  all our deaths
    unison of our last
      confusion
stopped breaths
  unison without blast
    or lambsblood bath
      world without end

Socrates died so
  willingly Jesus
    not without a struggle
      gave up the ghost
and a mother pleases
  to smother her baby
    in the Bronx or the Urewera
      some other pillow

  brain-tissue splashed
   fractionally after
    the bullet-hole appeared
     in the gib. board
freesias and catheters
  perfumed the ward
   in a hospice for the dying
    the jumbo crashed

the Trump played on
  like a sea in my sleep
   or the thumb-stopped ear
    where my blood can listen
to the river of itself
  nobody rose calling
   deep to our deep
    last unison.

A REFUSAL TO READ POEMS OF JAMES K. BAXTER AT A PERFORMANCE IN HONOUR OF HIS MEMORY IN CRANMER SQUARE, CHRISTCHURCH

Jim, you won't mind, will you,
if I don't come to your party?
One death is enough, I won't kill you
over again, ritually,
being only one other poet
who knew you younger and never better,
I would hardly know under which hat or which crown
to salute you now —
bays, or myrtles, or thorns,
or which of them best adorns
that grave ambiguous brow.

The quandary's mine, yours too,
Jim, isn't there always too much
we don't understand, too much that we do?
Winged words need no crutch,
and I've none for you.

March, 1973

TANTALUS

Tantalus, Tantalus, how are you getting on,
up to your guilty neck in the black river,
nothing to drink or to eat for an ever gone
and an ever to be?
                    Tantalus,
pick yourself a plum.
                        Tantalus,
dip your chin, drink.
                      Tantalus,
what's wrong with you?
                          God,
he's hopeless!
              Tantalus!

AN ABOMINABLE TEMPER

H. A. H. Monro, 1814-1908, sometime Judge of the Native Land Court, New Zealand, writes to his daughter, Ada Morrison.

i

What little do I know?
Really very little indeed.
You suggest that I write it down.
Well, Ada, I shall try.
As much as I remember,
having forgotten the most.

We, whoever we are,
have seen the century out.
So conveniently, I might
have gone, that hundredth Hogmanay.
Raw 1901
is a socket my tongue touches

unhopefully. I take up my pen,
not without a little pain.
A hard frost again this morning,
a sharp frost, needle to the bone
as I crook my knuckle to the pen,
a black frost. I dip and scratch
like an old fowl. Winter

comes last for us all.
A fogged window, the gaslight
fizzing in the afternoon —
I feel the steel nib searching
skull bone, wrist bone.
Having forgotten the most,
dear Ada, I am writing it down,

the little of what I was told
by my father and my mother,
by this last light in my mind,
blue bead on a black wick,
which leaves most things dark.
I think my grandfather was killed

in a sea battle. Trafalgar?
Why not, if it suits you?
Any other battle would do.
This winter light's too dim
for embroidering by,
supposing I had the talent.

ii

I am writing it down, as you say,
for my children and grandchildren,
or to oblige you, Ada.
I dip, and scratch.
What judgments did I scratch?
What claims? Whose lands?

Maori lands, when I was judge?
I am writing about my father.
He had an abominable temper —
That's written now.
When only a small boy,
he was taken to sea by his father,

the naval officer, who hoped
for a son in the same service.
In fact, he detested it.
I've often said, no wonder,
if the father and son were cursed
with the same bad temper.

Did my father hate his father
for a temper like his own?

No love was lost between him
and the sea, I'm sure of that.
I've often said, that first
voyage might have been his last —

I would not be sitting, Ada,
in this cold small city,
drizzling my winter away
out of the blinding mountains
into the blinded sea,
where the English trees don't care

what hemisphere this is
or month of the year,
and a hundred years are too
many, and too few.
I am writing about my father.
Quite a young man, he obtained

in his native Edinburgh,
some government situation.
I forget what, precisely.
I conclude it had a connexion
with the French wars, at all events
Waterloo was the end of it.
Othello's occupation was gone.

He could have had cash compensation
for the lost employment, or
he could name any colony for
his grant of land. The climate
in Tasmania was said to be healthy.
He sailed in the *Minerva*.

iii

Six months at sea, with my mother,
my brother William, my sister

Marie, — *tempestuous*.
I write down the one word
I ever heard of it.
I am sure, well chosen. It can hardly
have improved my father's temper.

But how promising it looked,
that Hobart landing!
Grass to the backs of the cattle
on the block my father chose.
It was her life's regret,
my mother would often say,

some blundering Sydney office
gave 400 trumpery acres,
Robinson's to my father,
and his fine block to Robinson.
Greener than the grass, my father
abandoned his rightful claim,

took money and lost a fortune.
He gained, in spite of it all,
a friend, Lieutenant Gunn,
ex-Imperial Army,
six foot six in his socks,
Commandant of Birch's Bay
convict station. Gunn

made me his special pet,
danced me on his knee.
A bushranger shot his arm off.
My father had his post,
with convict servants and all,
an eight-oared gig on the Derwent,
and a home rent free,

till the timber trade failed.
My father sailed
his own twenty-ton cutter
over to New Zealand.
Hell upon earth he found
at the Bay of Islands.
Hokianga, on the contrary,
agreeably surprised him,

the Maori a better class,
and so were the settlers,
several of them retired
army and navy officers,
highly respectable people
residing at Hokianga.

iv

My father found a purchaser there
for the twenty-ton cutter,
Count Dillon, a British sea-captain,
who obtained his title of Count
from a grateful French Government
for some service or other connected

with the mystery of La Perouse's
expedition. Just what, precisely,
escapes me. He was a Count,
a reward, I am sure, as gratifying
to him, as it was inexpensive
to France. Back again to Hobart

my father sailed in a trading schooner,
chartered the brig *Brazil Packet*,
captain and crew, took us all aboard
for New Zealand. So far, dear Ada,
so near, perhaps I should say,
I have picked my thread for you,

my child, my other children,
your children, their children,
great-grandchildren of mine,
among others, Arnold, John, Allen,
great-great-grandsons Wystan, Timothy, Simon.
I dip, and scratch the hyphens,

not without a little pain
the steel nib searches
wrist bone, skull bone,
testicles, time stitches
hyphen by hyphen this hand-me-down
garment we wear in our turn,

shrunk in the wash, or threadbare.
I am twitched from behind
as I crook my knuckle to the pen.
I am writing about my father.
Peace to his loins, dust somewhere now
in San Francisco. The last voyage,
of which I write nothing.

v

A mouth made mountainous with mere sand
if ever dung yellow dunes were mountains
opened that morning to suck our ship in.

Out of many inlets, branches, root-breathers
of mangroves intaking, expelling pungent air,
a little strong for my taste now, not then,

mucus of a strange mother smeared us over
from head to foot. We were not visitors there
but visceral as hydatid worm to host.

Underfoot at Horeke the ground swayed civilly,
steadied, at the suggestion of our steps.
We lugged our worldly goods ashore,

> *item* tables and chairs
> *item* window sashes and doors (2)
> *item* bricks for the chimneys
> *item* one ton of flour
> *item* a team of four bullocks (£100)
> *item* a cart
> *item* a plough
> *item* harrows

On a block of land bought from the natives
the erection of a dwelling-house proceeded,
my mother, my two sisters and I meanwhile

accommodated in the house of a settler.
No sooner built than burned to the ground,
all our possessions with it. An accident,

at least I never heard anyone blamed for it.
My mother and sisters stayed on with the settler,
my father and I, my brother, our boy interpreter

(till more supplies could be obtained from Hobart)
roughed it in a hut the Maoris built for us,
one room, provided with

> *item* one frying-pan
> *item* four halves of coconut shell for cups
> *item* mussel shells stuck on reeds for spoons

Clearing the land went on, a hundred Maoris
were employed on this. If I remember rightly,
the daily wage was half a fig of tobacco —

eighteen figs to the pound, sixpence per pound.
Labour was not dear in those days.
Not that as a child that would have occurred to me.

Burned to the ground, a smouldering heap
heaves into memory, he and his household goods,
cold ashes now. This charred fag-end of me

pokes here and there. All fires are accidents,
if one happens to be ninety years of age,
most accidents have done, as we say they will.

vi

Re-supplied from Hobart, my father had built
a large weatherboard house, outhouses, boatshed.
He enclosed several acres and made a garden.

Like the Garden of Eden, I am tempted to say.
If it had been less like — indeed, dear Ada,
you know your Bible, I hope, as well as I do.

Yes, it was a pleasant life at Hokianga,
only for my father's abominable temper
we could have been very happy,

with a hundred head of cattle, as many goats,
innumerable pigs, fowls, geese, ducks, turkeys,
a beautiful six-oared gig rowed by six Maoris

(boys, we called those in our regular employ)
and the shooting and fishing. My father kept
his bad temper entirely for home consumption,

outside his family he never quarrelled with anyone.
The bad times came, the garden went
the way of all gardens from the first, I suppose.

Depression swept the Colonies,
Australia bankrupt, New Zealand fallen to zero.
Sails were few and listless on the Hokianga.

Disobedient to my father,
the timber trade failed again, the Maoris felled
no more kauri to make him spars for Chile.

Heke took an axe to the Flagstaff instead,
at the Bay of Islands. The War in the North began.
My father chartered a ship, the barque *Bolina*,

to carry us all, with his other belongings,
including the hundred cattle, south to Auckland.
I grew to manhood, married, you and the rest

came into the world. I write nothing of that.
Last light leaves most things dark, the nearer
the darker. Our secrets keep themselves.

vii

Did he love nobody?
Nobody him? Dear Ada,
I do not imagine my father
got me in a fit of temper,
whatever the connexion was.
Such things, if possible at all,
one prefers to think unlikely.

Can you, yourself, imagine
what the feeling was, my feeling
when my semen left me lonely
and you lonelier?
An absurd question. Precisely,
or I should not ask it.

Ask God why he does such things.

viii

Was he of a romantic disposition?
Peter I mean, my father.
Born the same year as Keats
who shuddered at the sight of old women,
horrors! they knew too much,

and peppered his tongue
to taste the claret better,
I am sure he was otherwise preoccupied
in his native Edinburgh.

Was it smelly between the sheets?

What in the name of God and Robbie Burns
and the nine merry Muses was he doing
at Hokianga, not caring half a fig
of tobacco while the timber was profitable,
he with his gentlemanly tastes,
and the better class he never quarrelled with,
cherishing besides

item   one pair brass-barrelled black-nippled
         spring-daggered percussion duelling pistols
item   one *Poems* of Robert Burns, Edinburgh, 1812
item   one Holy Bible?

ix

My mother's maiden name was Alcock,
grand-daughter of an Englishman.
County family. It took his butler
all day to clean the silver plate.
He in his dotage left the estate
to some other relative.
                    This fool
of a grandmother of mine! My mother
was robbed, the second time, of a fortune.

My mother's younger sister Jane
died, unmarried, long, long ago.

x

In the beginning was the four letter Word
Tetragrammaton, an angry father.
The pistols will be sold for fifty pounds
by my grandson Tremayne to Arthur Morten,
collector of old firearms, whose collection
will pass on his death to the Canterbury Museum,
Christchurch, New Zealand.
Allen will get the Bible and the *Poems*.

I speak as a fool, fools shall repeat after me.

This prophecy Allen *shall make,
for I live before his time.*

NOTES

NOTES

ENEMIES

'MOUNTAIN ELEGY' was suggested by the Suite in B Minor for Flutes and Strings, of J. S. Bach. The first two parts were intended to follow the *grave* leading to *allegro*, and the *sarabande*, of the suite. But the poem developed of itself and on advice I deleted musical terms which I had used to separate the parts of the poem. — 1937. It must not appear that I knew the music musically. Among the few recordings I possessed in those pre-stereo days one was of this suite, played by the Concertgebouw orchestra of Amsterdam. I cannot remember any that I listened to nearly so often, or that delighted me more. It was in my mind's ear distinctly while I wrote the poem. Somebody may remember the charming verse mimicry of a *gigue* in J. C. Beaglehole's *Considerations on Certain Music of J. S. Bach*. I knew his poem, but what happened in my case was quite different, if only because I did not have his pianist's privilege and skill; if I was naive, it was not in supposing I could write verse that might accompany such music, only that the poem depended on the music, as I am sure it did. — 1973.

ISLAND AND TIME

THE UNHISTORIC STORY. 'The Land of Beach . . . ' This reference, with others in the same poem, I have from J. C. Beaglehole's *Exploration of the Pacific*. From 17th century Dutch sources the author gives examples of the current belief in the existence of a fabulously rich country or continent somewhere in the south. Frederick de Houtman, coming on the west coast of Australia, thought 'that this must be the coastline of the "Beach" or "Locach" of Marco Polo, with its fabulous riches.' Visscher, Tasman's chief adviser, planned the discovery of 'all the utterly unknown provinces of Beach.' Gold was thought to be abundant there, and some hoped to profit by the inhabitants' supposed ignorance of its value. — 1941.

ST THOMAS'S RUINS. By the St Helier's Bay road, Auckland, there stood in an open paddock the ruined and roofless walls of a small imitation-Gothic church, known as St Thomas's Ruins.

The church is said to have been built by Bishop Selwyn, nostalgic for a place of worship recalling the stone churches of England. But it was ill-constructed; the mortar did not hold, so people said, because it was mixed with sea-sand. Selwyn's timber churches, like the St John's College chapel near by, have lasted 120 years and longer; ironically, this stone structure failed, and had been abandoned for many years when I first knew it in 1931. Since the poem was written, the ruin has been replaced, with no great loss, by a characterless stone building after a local builder's conception of church design. — 1941, 1973.

THE VICTIM. Though this poem requires no note, I wish here to acknowledge a debt to J. C. Beaglehole's *Discovery of New Zealand*. I owe the occasion, if not the impulse, and most of the material of this poem, to his account of Tasman's voyage and the portion of Tasman's journal quoted by him. — 1941.

SAILING OR DROWNING

LANDFALL IN UNKNOWN SEAS was written during 1942, and before the year ended, Douglas Lilburn had composed the music for strings which so splendidly complements and illuminates the verse. Both were undertaken for the Natural Historical Branch of the Department of Internal Affairs. What this really means is that the late J. C. Beaglehole, O.M., asked me to write a poem about Tasman's voyage, to be part of the commemorative volume designed by him for its tercentenary. This book, *Abel Janszoon Tasman and the Discovery of New Zealand*, was produced by the Department for official and private distribution; it was entirely John Beaglehole's conception, both as historian and typographical designer. It consisted of his own specially written essay with a new translation of Tasman's log, and the poem. When I had finished, I showed the poem to Lilburn, then living in the old brick apartment block on the site now occupied by the Christchurch Town Hall. I would have called, as I so often did, on my way to work at *The Press*. I hoped it would strike him as a subject for music. By great good fortune it did, though part of the fortune was (I am glad to think) that we knew each other's minds so well; no-one would have been quicker to perceive it, than Lilburn, if the poem and his music could not agree. With an immediate response from Beaglehole and from Joe (afterwards Sir Joseph) Heenan, then head of Internal Affairs, the music was completed and the first performance arranged; it took place in Wellington on 13 December 1942, three hundred years to the day since Tasman first sighted New Zealand. I have not counted the many performances since: at least one for each of the thirty years, including three in 1973. — 1973.

POEMS 1949-1957

IN MEMORY OF DYLAN THOMAS. When Dylan Thomas died in 1953, Charles Brasch asked me to write a memoir for *Landfall*. It was three years since Ruth Witt and I had seen Thomas off at the San Francisco airport: he returning east, and I, a few days later to sail for New Zealand. It was not the time, and perhaps not the place either, for me to attempt any connected account of what I had known of him, our meetings in London in 1949, a week with him in Wales the same year, our experiences together (memorable enough, though not much in the way of stories that have lost too little in the telling) in America during 1950. The poem sprang from the feeling that I was not let off. It appeared in *Landfall*, with some photographs for sufficient explanation that it was written in part from personal recollection. When it was reprinted in *A Garland for Dylan Thomas* (New York, 1963) I added a brief note in place of the photographs. Neither should be needed today; but I remember a friend's warning, that some readers might mistake me: there was such a flood of poetic tributes in those years. — 1973.

TREES, EFFIGIES, MOVING OBJECTS

If I say these poems were written in the spring and summer of 1971-2, I mean that is when they were finished and found the order in which they now appear. A poet never stops trying to save poetry from poetry, to make something of it, not a spurious everything.

Memory is always something, but if memory were ever good enough—even of a moment ago!—would we want poetry? Isn't this the necessary irritant? Because of it, memory is a thing of the present, a thing of the future too, if that is not already taken care of. Why should the irritant, in a particular spring and summer, fasten on these few things, not any of the many other conceivable *those*? The missing poem, the one that didn't get written, might have answered that. Has it perhaps got written after all? It ought to be the single poem of which these are the lines and the spaces. — 1972.